AGRICULTURAL REFORM IN INDIA

AGRICULTURAL REFORM IN INDIA.

BY

A. O. HUME, C. B.

GYAN

Published by

Gyan Publishing House
5, Ansari Road
Daryaganj, New Delhi-110002
Phone: 011-47034999, 9811692060
E-mail: books@gyanbooks.com

Distribution Network
gyanbooks.com
India, USA, Canada, UK, Australia

ISBN: 978-81-212-5981-1 (PB)
First Published, 1879

2nd Impression 2024

Printed at: Gyan Press, Delhi.

AGRICULTURAL REFORM IN INDIA
Author: A. O. HUME

AGRICULTURAL REFORM IN INDIA.

BY

A. O. HUME, C.B.,

LATE SECRETARY TO THE GOVERNMENT OF INDIA IN THE DEPARTMENT OF REVENUE, AGRICULTURE, AND COMMERCE.

LONDON:

W. H. ALLEN & CO., 13 WATERLOO PLACE,

PALL MALL, S.W.

PUBLISHERS TO THE INDIA OFFICE.

1879.

PREFACE.

This paper, written many months ago, had been long in type, when the Government emphasised many of the remarks that it contains by abolishing altogether the Department of Agriculture.

This Department has never, as fully explained in this pamphlet, been able to effect much where Agriculture was concerned, but it was working in a right direction; it knew what was required, and from time to time, when allowed a chance, did a little good on its own motion, or supported and assisted the efforts of others in this direction.

So long as it existed, there was always some one at the Head-quarters of the Government of India who possessed a knowledge of these subjects, and was at hand to support and advocate the sanction of all reasonable and practicable projects for improving in any way, however humble, the Agriculture of the country. So long as it existed, there was always a hope, that amid the vicissitudes to which public affairs are subject, some lucky turn of the wheel might bring more enlightened ideas on these subjects into vogue, and thus render possible its conversion into a real, working AGRICULTURAL BUREAU.

All this has passed away, and the only hope for India now lies in the chance that the real bearings and vital importance of the questions herein discussed may be better understood and appreciated in England than they have ever been, since Lord Mayo's death, by those in power in India.

A. O. HUME.

SIMLA,
July 1*st*, 1879.

AGRICULTURAL REFORM IN INDIA.

RECENT and oft-recurring famines have revived, to a slight extent, the feeble interest which has occasionally, in past times, been evinced in regard to agriculture in India.

Some few people are found who ask whether improved husbandry might not do much to mitigate the intensity and limit the areas of these calamities.

Others, looking to India's present impecuniosity, to the difficulties involved in any very material reduction in her present expenditure, to the urgent necessities that must arise in the future for increased expenditure, to the comparatively slow growth of existing sources of revenue and the apparent impracticability of opening out new sources that her populations would accept without dangerous dissatisfaction, enquire whether the time has not come for a careful reconsideration of our management of the land of the country. The land revenue in all historical periods has been the main financial resource of every successive Government, Hindoo or Mahomedan. We have done much for the country, have enormously increased the value of its produce, yet province for province we are not receiving much more than many of our predecessors, Akbar for instance, did. Are we really making the most out of the land?

Philanthropic manufacturers of agricultural machines, introducers of new forage plants, patentees of improved cattle food and the like, overcome by the woes of the Indian ryot, are perpetually dinning into the ears of the authorities and the public their unselfish anxiety to regenerate the country by supplying it with their wares on a large scale.

One way or another a dim conception seems to be gaining ground that, perhaps, we have left well (or ill?) alone too long, and that possibly a systematic improvement in its agriculture might prove a remedy for many of India's present troubles.

This is not the first time that some little stir has been made about this matter. The orbit is not calculable, but a certain periodicity has been observed, and every ten or fifteen years the idea has emerged into the blaze of public opinion. Whether this time it is destined to develop into a permanent source of light, or once more, its perihelion passed, to dart off into the space of oblivion, cannot be foretold. The chances are, it is to be feared, greatly in favour of the latter; but who can tell? The laws of mind are not as those of matter; and anyhow, so long as a chance exists, all, however humble, who hope and believe—hope that at last the time may have arrived for energetic and sufficient action in this matter, and believe that that action will confer great and lasting benefits on a considerable fraction of mankind—are bound, so far as in them lies, to endeavour to lead others to the same hope and belief.

Most certainly the question, are we making the most out of the land, must be answered in the negative; but this, not through any imperfection in the existing revenue administration, but because the land itself yields nothing like what it should.

It is undeniable that in the tenures we have created, and the systems we have adopted, there have been grave errors. Take, for instance, the Permanent Settlement of Bengal. Here, as elsewhere in India, the ruling power was the sole proprietor of the land. Other people enjoyed various classes of occupancy rights, and could not, according to custom, be deprived of these (though they often were so by our predecessors) so long as they continued to pay the demand of the ruling power, which again, though in practice often only limited by rebellion, ought to have been, according to tradition, one-sixth of the gross produce, or again, which according to custom is the same thing, one-half of what the actual cultivator paid the middleman who made the collections. No doubt over vast tracts the produce was nominally equally divided between cultivator and middleman (*adh-buttai* as this division is called), but as a matter of fact, owing to the frauds of the cultivators, we may say broadly, that these never did over any large area, for any prolonged period, yield more than one-third of the gross produce to the State collectors, middlemen, zemindars, &c. who, in various parts of the empire, at various periods, have been the primary recipients of the dues of the soil.

It would be foreign to my present purpose to enter further into details here. Suffice it to say that the State, even if strictly adhering to traditional usage, retained the right to share in any increased productiveness in its property, and similarly to increase the tale of its demand if *prices* of produce rose, or the value of the currency fell.

In Bengal, with the most laudable intentions, we relinquished this right. We began by fixing a demand higher than the existing condition of affairs justified according to traditional theory, but not higher than what our immediate predecessors had taken, and this demand we stereotyped for ever.

Time has rolled on; a roadless wilderness has been traversed in all directions by railways and roads; under our protecting rule a vast internal and foreign commerce has been developed, prices of agricultural produce have risen, new and extremely remunerative staples have been introduced, and vast tracts of waste have come under the plough, but our demand remains the same as it was seventy years ago, and is probably between four and five* millions less than it

---

* It will be doubtless urged that, according to the road cess returns, the gross rental is barely 13 millions, and that therefore at the outside the Government demand could not have exceeded $6\frac{1}{2}$ millions, or say $3\frac{1}{4}$ millions in excess of its present amount. The writer, on the other hand, is confident, looking to area, soils, rates, and population that the "assets" of Bengal, as calculated for a North-West Province settlement, are not under 16 millions, and probably exceed this considerably.

Years ago, when the Bengal population was assumed at from 40 to 44 millions, the writer, from similar considerations, asserted in a printed memorandum to Government that it could not be

would have been at the present moment had our predecessors contented themselves in Bengal, as elsewhere, with fixing the demand for periods of twenty or thirty years.

These extra millions would have made the administration easy. We should never have heard of license and income taxes, hateful to the country, however equitable in theory; famine expenditure would not, as now, have involved proximate insolvency, and nine-tenths of the fiscal measures of the last fifteen years, which have created a more or less sore feeling in every section and grade of the community, would have been unnecessary.

Had the country gained by it, we might derive some consolation in looking back on this stupendous error. But the result has been only to create a multitude of absentee landlords and rent-charge holders, and to leave the masses, except in particular localities,* worse off and more miserable than those of any other part of the empire.

Again, throughout large tracts elsewhere, we have created middlemen and converted into joint proprietors with ourselves men formerly only representatives of a community, men anciently only *primi inter pares*, collecting for a small *honorarium* the dues of their

---

less than 60 millions. Everybody ridiculed the idea, and many excellent jokes were made at his expense, *but*, three years later, the first census was taken, and the population was proved to be 66 millions.

* The Mahomedan cultivators of Eastern Bengal, whose turbulent pugnacity has enabled them to hold their own to a certain extent, must be excepted.

brethren, now lording it as masters, and intercepting one-half of the State dues.

In these and similar cases we are doubtless *not* now getting by perhaps eight millions a year as much as we might have done, but for the well-meant errors of our predecessors. But these are accomplished facts; they have been built into the very foundations of the new social order that has arisen under our rule, and no wise or competent ruler could now dream of changes in these directions. For good or for evil, there they are, and there they must remain, unless we desire to shake society to its base and risk the overthrow of the fabric on which three generations have laboured.

Broadly speaking, accepting these tenures and systems that we have created, and of which we *cannot* and *must* not even *try* to rid ourselves, it may be safely asserted that we *are* making as much on the whole out of the land as, in its present condition, we can.

It is only necessary, at any rate for those who understand these questions, to read the more recent Settlement Reports of any of the temporarily-settled provinces, such as Bombay, the North-Western Provinces, the Punjab, to realise the patience and research, the care and intelligence, with which the assessment of the Government land revenue is now conducted.

Certainly, making due allowance where settlements have been running for some time, for improvements that railways, canals, and other less direct causes have effected in the value of produce, as a whole we are taking as much from the land as we can, consistently with not injuring the capital value of our property. Like all great works, the workmanship varies somewhat in quality, and it is only in human nature to err at times. Districts, both somewhat under and somewhat over assessed, might easily be indicated, but taking a wide purview no competent authority can deny that, conditioned as it is by the irrevocable acts of the past, the land revenue administration is, on the whole, making as much out of the land as it can fairly be expected, as now worked, to yield to Government.

If, then, our revenue from land is to undergo any very marked development, and to bear hereafter that proportion to the rest of our revenues that in the times gone by it has always borne, it is to an increase in the produce of the land, to an improved system of agriculture in fact, that we must look.

And here it is due to the patient, frugal, and not unintelligent husbandmen of India to admit freely that, looking to the conditions under which they labour, their ignorance of scientific method, and their want of capital (and all that capital enables a farmer to command), the crops that they do produce are, on the whole, surprising.

So far as rule-of-thumb goes, the experience of 3,000 years has not been wholly wasted. They know to a day when it is best (if only meteorological conditions permit) to sow each staple and each variety of each staple that is grown in their neighbourhood; they know the evils of banks and hedges, dwarfing the crops on either side and harbouring vermin, and will have none of them; they accurately distinguish every* variety of soil, and, so far as the crops they grow are concerned, the varying properties and capacities of each; they fully realise the value (though they can command but little) of ordinary manure, ashes, and the like, and recognise which are most required by which kind of crops; they know the advantages of ploughing, in most cases as deep as their imperfect implements and feeble teams will permit, and of thoroughly pulverising the soil; and they also recognise where, with a scanty or no supply of manure, it would be folly to break the shallow-lying pan. As for weeds, their wheat-fields would, in this respect,

* Nothing, indeed, is more perplexing than the enormous number of names applied by native agriculturists to soils, the more so that probably almost every district rejoices in at least a dozen purely local names which are unknown elsewhere. There is no real confusion, however. Native cultivators as keenly appreciate the smallest differences in the relative qualities of different soils as do the best European farmers, but the fact is that independent of names indicative of the quality of the soil (and often to the entire *exclusion* of these) they make use, in describing their land, of names having reference to external conditions, the frequency or recency of cultivation therein, its situation as regards inhabited sites, &c., its position as upland or recently-formed alluvium, its occupation for pasture, fields, or gardens, its external features, &c. &c. Nothing is more common than to hear soils referred to as such, by names which really only indicate features or circumstances altogether external to the soil itself and independent of its intrinsic quality. This is no doubt inaccurate, but it is very natural since the value to the agriculturist of any land will often depend far more on these external circumstances than on the inherent quality of the soil, which latter, moreover, will, as time goes on, be often greatly modified by the former, as where "*bhoor*" or light sandy soil, becomes in course of time, by proximity to a village, constant cultivation and manuring, a kind of "*do mut*" between garden mould and rich loam.

shame ninety-nine hundredths of those in Europe. You may stand on some high old barrow-like village site in Upper India, and look down on all sides on one wide sea of waving wheat broken only by dark-green islands of mango groves—many, many square miles of wheat and not a weed or blade of grass above six inches in height to be found amongst it. What is to be spied out creeping here and there on the ground is only the growth of the last few weeks, since the corn grew too high and thick to permit the women and children to continue weeding. They know when to feed down a too forward crop; they know the benefit of, and practise, so far as circumstances and poverty permit, a rotation of crops. They are great adepts in storing grain, and will turn it out of rough earthen pits, after twenty years, absolutely uninjured. They know the exact state of ripeness to which grain should be allowed to stand in different seasons; in other words, under different meteorological conditions, to ensure its *keeping* when thus stored; and equally the length of time that, under varying atmospheric conditions, it should lie upon the open threshing-floor to secure the same object.

Imperfect appliances, superstition, money troubles, and the usurer's impatience, often prevent their practising what they do know, but so far as what may be called non-scientific agriculture is concerned, there is little to teach them, and certainly very few European farmers could, fettered by the same conditions as our ryots, produce better, if as good, crops.

On the other hand, we must not over-rate their knowledge; it is wholly empirical, and is in many parts of the country, if not everywhere, greatly limited in its application by tradition and superstition. Innumerable quaint couplets, to which a certain reverence is attached, deal with agricultural matters. These, in Upper India at any rate, are true "household words" amongst all tillers of the soil. These govern their actions to a great extent, and often lead them wrong against their better judgment. They take omens of all kinds to guide their choice of crops and other operations of husbandry, and though some few of the more intelligent only act upon the results of these divinations when they coincide with their own views, the masses are blindly guided by them.

So, then, it is not only external disadvantages against which the Indian cultivator has to contend, it is not only that his knowledge is still in the primary experience stage, but that even this knowledge is often rendered of no avail by the traditions of an immemorial religion of agriculture.

It is necessary to realise* this (of which few Europeans ever even hear), as it is one great practical difficulty against which agricultural reform in India will have to contend.

What other Government is so favoured as that of India? A fertile soil, and nine-tenths of it (excluding Lower Bengal) still so far the property of the State, that the latter can, and does, levy a full rent on all

---

* To give some more definite idea of this superstition, a brief extract from an unpublished Memoir on the Agriculture of the Doab is reproduced as Note A., at the close of this paper.

of it—a rent which it can periodically enhance as circumstances enable the land to bear it.

And yet we are always in difficulty about money.* Conceive the Government of Great Britain similarly situated, and yet having to levy income taxes, and license taxes, and the like.

Well may the people of India cry out against innovations like these, and say, "the State keeps all the land in the country; this ought to suffice for any Government; if it does not, the Government, whatever its other merits, is too dear at the price." And this *is* the feeling that is slowly, but surely, creeping over the face of the empire. It is not the confirmed malcontents only, these must always be numerous in a country governed by foreigners; it is equally those best affected to our rule who begin to say, "The Government means well, it does much for us, it gives us peace internally, but this is a poor country, and the Government costs too much!"

We must be blind indeed to the teachings of history if we cannot, to some extent, foretell to what this must ultimately lead.

Now that the people feel so keenly the costliness of the Government is due in some degree to unwise and unnecessary expenditure,† but mainly to the fact that our land revenue, not having advanced in proportion

---

* The writer can remember no period within the last twenty years, when any attempts to obtain funds for agricultural improvements were not negatived on the ground of financial pressure.

† This is too large a question to enter on here, though one branch of it has been glanced at in a later portion of this paper.

to the growth in other directions of the empire, money has had to be raised in ways which, however equitable in principle, are opposed to the traditions and repugnant to the feelings of the people.

Were our land revenue now only thirty instead of twenty-two millions, our expenditure might be precisely what it is, and yet no one, malcontent or otherwise, would ever have grumbled. All the money we needed would have been obtained by what the people consider constitutional and legitimate means, and so long as we adhered to old-established lines and introduced no new forms of taxation (and we should have needed none had our land revenue been what it should) we were welcome to spend all we got and, for all the masses cared, how we pleased.

That our land revenue has not kept pace with the general development is due to two causes:—

The first, mistakes in system, already alluded to—mistakes now irremediable.

The second, our absolute neglect, though sole or part proprietors of the major portion of the land, to attempt the smallest improvement on a primitive system of agriculture, stereotyped two thousand years ago, when the conditions and requirements of the country were utterly unlike what they are now, and when scientific method was undreamt of.

So long as we hold the country and see a fair prospect of continuing to hold it for another quarter of a century, it can never be too late to repair this second error, and the sooner we boldly face the necessity of doing this, and take action on a scale commensurate with the greatness of the task, the sooner we shall extricate ourselves from the trying position in which we are now placed, and relieve the country of troubles mainly due to our own past, unintentional, mismanagement.

And here the reader may possibly think that some injustice is being done to our administration, and remembering that eight years or so ago a good deal was heard of the establishment, under Lord Mayo's auspices, of an Agricultural Department in India, may ask how the existence of this special department is compatible with such an entire neglect of agricultural reform as has been asserted.

The answer is simple: There is not, and never has been, any real Agricultural Department in India. There is a Miscellaneous Department of the Government of India, which, amongst its various titles, bears the word "Agriculture," but that Department has not, and cannot, from the nature of things, exercise any potential influence on the agriculture of the country *quoad* which it is a *vox et præterea nihil.*

Nothing is more calculated to deter earnest men from exerting themselves to secure for India that agricultural development of which she stands so grievously in need than the belief (erroneous as it is) that there already exists a special local organisation for this very purpose, and I propose, therefore, to explain—

What the so-called Agricultural Department really does;

How, though bearing this title, it has done, and (as at present constituted) can do, nothing (worthy the name) to reform Indian agriculture;

What organisation is necessary to any real and efficient Department of Agriculture in India, and the urgent need in which the country stands of this.

Lastly I shall, by way of illustration, glance at some few of the more important problems that would probably, at the outset, engage the attention of any such Department.

I.

What the so-called Department of Agriculture really does and has done.

Although circumstances (to be explained later) had deprived Lord Mayo's new department of all claim to be considered an Agricultural Bureau, its formation marked an era in the history of the country, and served a most useful purpose. In it were gathered up into one homogeneous whole numberless branches of the administration, all more or less potential factors in the material progress of the empire. Branches, therefore, scattered amongst the different secretariats of the Government of India, to be attended to or not, as the more obligatory business of these secretariats might, from time to time, permit; and when obtaining attention, dealt with too often by officers necessarily possessing neither the special knowledge nor the experience essential to their satisfactory direction.

The administration of the Forest Department was transferred from the Public Works Secretariat, and with it the immediate control of a large staff. This involved the general direction of the demarcation, conservation, and improvement of all State forests in the Bengal Presidency, of the supply of timber and firewood to State Departments and the general public, of the formation of new plantations, the *reboisment* of denuded tracts, and the other very varied operations of this extensive Department.*

From the Military Department was transferred all business connected with studs and horse-breeding. From the Financial Department the supervision of the Department of Inland Customs, and salt matters generally, including all correspondence connected—at first with the maintenance and guard, and later with the gradual abolition,† of the vast customs' barrier, then extending across the continent of India from above Attock to near Cuttack; with the working of the great salt mines in the Punjab and the Sambhur

---

* Although the Secretary possesses some knowledge of forestry, and has co-operated cordially with Colonel Pearson, Mr. Baden-Powell, and Dr. Brandis, who have successively (the first two officiating) held under him the office of Inspector-General of Forests, the real credit for the enormous progress effected in forest administration, since the formation of the Revenue, Agriculture, and Commerce Department, is primarily due to Dr. Brandis, the founder, in India, of scientific forestry.

† This, though the proposal was of old standing, and the measure has received the approval, and more or less the support, of Lords Lawrence, Mayo, Northbrook, and Lytton, was more especially the Secretary's work. Its feasibility depended on the negotiation of a series of treaties with numerous native states. Writing of this recently, the Secretary of State remarked (Despatch No. 3 of 6th February 1879, para. 8) :—" I entirely concur in the high appreciation of Mr. Hume's long and valuable services expressed by your Excellency's Government; for to him, as you observe, is due the initiation, prosecution, and completion of that policy which has led to the agreements entered into with the several states concerned."

lake, and with all measures relating to the security and development of the salt revenue in India, and the reduction of the price of this necessary to consumers.

From the Foreign Department was taken over the control of all matters connected with Land Revenue and Settlements in the non-regulation provinces; and from the Home Department all similar work pertaining to the regulation provinces.

The business thus devolving on the new Department included all questions connected with the settlement and assessment of the land in all that portion of India which is not permanently settled (*i.e.* nearly the whole empire with the exception of the major portion of Lower Bengal and the Benares division); all questions connected with waste lands, and their grant in lease or fee-simple to European and other settlers; all questions connected with the alienation of the State revenue derived from the land; all questions connected with the imposition of local taxes and cesses on the land, and later, when an Act was passed providing for the making of pecuniary advances by the State to aid the landholder or cultivator in improving his land, all questions connected with the working of that Act.

From the Home Department also, the following other branches of work were transferred :—

Surveys.—Under this head were included the direction of the Trigonometrical, Topographical, Revenue, and Geological Surveys, and the administration of the vast establishments charged with their execution. Connected with the Geological Survey were explorations for minerals,—coal, petroleum, &c., and the grant of leases and concessions to individuals or companies desirous of searching for, or working these in various parts of the country.

Industry, Science, and Art.—Including questions connected with the representation of India at Exhibitions in Europe, America, and Australia; the holding of art and other exhibitions in this country; the general control of museums of natural history and economic products of such scientific matters as the maintenance of astronomical observatories and the arrangements for observing solar eclipses, the transit of Venus, and securing daily photographs of the sun; also all questions connected with industrial products, and the encouragement and development of local industries.

Meteorology.—Including the administration of the Meteorological Department, and the initiation and control of a system for the regular record and weekly or daily publication of reports on atmospheric variations and the prospects of the seasons.

Agriculture and Horticulture.—Including the general direction and control of model and experimental farms and botanic gardens; the introduction of new products, and of improved varieties of those already grown in the country; the introduction of new implements, and the improvement of those used by cultivators; the improvement of stock, and the prevention and cure of cattle disease; the conduct of operations connected with the cultivation of chinchona and the preparation from its bark of a really cheap and efficient febrifuge.

Fibres and Silk.—Including all questions connected with the improvement of the quality of Indian cotton, and the development of the trade in it; the improvement and development of Indian silk, the produce of the domesticated as well as of the wild worms; the introduction of suitable machinery for the treatment of rheea; the development of paper-making from fibres grown in the country, and the experimental cultivation of new or hitherto little known and neglected fibres.

Fisheries.—The whole of the inland and sea fisheries of the different provinces of India were systematically inspected and reported upon under the orders of this department, and measures taken, where necessary, in communication with Local Governments, for their conservation. A scientific manual of Indian Fishes by Dr. Day was also arranged for and has been published.

Port Blair and the Nicobars.—The administration of these settlements was vested in this department, and remained with it for over a year and a half, when, for reasons of administrative convenience, the work was retransferred to the Home Department.

Sanitation.—Questions connected with rural, urban, and army sanitation, and the organisation and working of the Sanitary Department, and the administration of lock hospitals. This work was retransferred about twenty-seven months later to the Home Department.

Municipalities.—Including all questions connected with municipal taxation and municipal government generally; the making of loans to municipalities for the execution of projects of local improvement, and cognate matters. This work was, after five and a half years, retransferred to the Home Department.

Emigration.—Including the regulation and control of emigration from India to British and Foreign colonies, and correspondence connected with the treatment of the emigrants there, and their return to India; also all correspondence connected with emigration to the tea districts of Assam, and State schemes of emigration, such as the emigration from Bengal to Burmah in 1874, during the famine in Behar, and the emigration of agriculturists to the Central Provinces from other over-populated tracts.

Statistics.—Operations connected with the Weights and Measures Act (a dead letter), the taking of the census of India, and the preparation of a Gazetteer, based on the results of an elaborate statistical survey.

To all these departments were added:—

In 1874—All correspondence connected with merchant shipping, lights, buoys, and beacons, ports and port dues, pilots and pilotage.

In the same year—The administration of a new department then constituted for the purpose of surveying systematically all the coasts and harbours of India, issuing charts of the same to the public, publishing hydrographic notices and notices of dangers to navigation, and changes in positions of lights and buoys, registers of wrecks, and accounts of lighthouses and light-vessels.

In 1875—The compilation of statistics of trade, seaborne and inland, for the whole empire, their collation and prompt publication, with explanatory notices and reviews of the figures, involving detailed enquiries into the commercial and industrial aspects of the country.

In 1876—The administration of the sea customs revenue, bringing with it the control of all the custom houses, and the discussion of all matters connected with the tariff of import and export duties.

II.

Why the Agricultural Department has not done, and never can do (as at present constituted), anything material for the improvement of Indian Agriculture.

The organisation essential to any efficient Bureau of Agriculture, and the urgent need in which India stands of such a department.

The above brief *résumé* of the work with which the Department of Revenue, Agriculture, and Commerce has been charged, and of the very numerous subjects dealt with in it, might, to a certain extent, be held to explain why so little, comparatively, has been done where agriculture is concerned.

It might, with much show of reason, be argued that with such an inordinate variety of questions to deal with, with such a vast mass of operations of the most diverse kinds, to direct, control, or supervise, no small department, with a single Secretary and Under Secretary, could possibly find time, after disposing of current work that inevitably came before it, to make new work, such as any effective action in the direction of agricultural improvement must involve.

This explanation, this argument, however valid *per se*, would not fully or sufficiently state the case.

Despite its heavy normal work, this Department *has* found the time to introduce more or less important reforms in the majority of the other branches with which it is supposed to deal. It has continually, and it is believed usefully, made new work for itself and carried out that work. It is in agriculture only that the Department, conceived originally mainly as an instrument for agricultural reform, has done next to nothing, and the reasons for this lamentable anomaly are to be sought for in causes widely different from the mere pressure of other work.

Though originally designated the Department of Agriculture, &c., this Department has never, from the first, been so constituted as to permit of its dealing either directly or efficiently with agricultural matters.

Lord Mayo's conception was one thing, the sadly modified scheme that as the result of vehement opposition he was compelled to accept, another. Lord Mayo accepted this as a sort of instalment, as a grant of ground on which he might later build what was necessary, but no one was more thoroughly alive to the fact than himself, that in the shape in which his cherished project ultimately saw the light, it afforded little or no prospect of material improvement in agriculture. He believed that in a few years this might all be changed, and had he lived, this might have been so, but he fully realised the position, and his invariable reply to protests on this subject were: "We must have patience; it will all come right."

Lord Mayo clung, however, to the idea of ultimately making this really a Department of Agriculture, but the Secretary of State did not approve of even this.

Lord Mayo named it the Department of Agriculture, Revenue, and Commerce. The Secretary of State objected to this, said that Revenue, and not Agriculture, was the main object of the Department, and ordered the name to be altered* to "Revenue, Agriculture, and Commerce."

Lord Mayo selected as head of the Department, an officer whom, from his own thorough† knowledge of the subject, he ascertained to be well versed in practical European agriculture, who had, for his own information and amusement, farmed in a small experi-

---

* Extract paras. 3 and 4 of a despatch (No. 27 of the 3rd August 1871) of Her Majesty's Secretary of State for India, to His Excellency the Governor-General of India in Council.

"3. I consider, however, that the change that has been made in the designation enjoined in paragraph 20 of my despatch of the 22nd September 1870, No. 61, by transposing the words Revenue and Agriculture, is objectionable, as giving rise to the notion that the revenue subjects, which are undoubtedly of the first importance, are not so esteemed by the authorities in this country or in India. Of such paramount importance are these subjects, that it is obviously necessary that the officer appointed to the post of Secretary in this Department should always be chosen on account of his knowledge of the subjects connected with revenue, rather than from any knowledge which he may possess of agricultural or commercial matters.

"4. I must, therefore, direct you to revert to the title settled by my despatch above alluded to, which, indeed, is the designation most frequently made use of by your Excellency in Council in the Resolution of the 6th of June."

† Lord Mayo was probably the only Governor-General who has farmed for a livelihood and made a living out of it. When he came of age (he was then Mr. Bourke), his father (whose elder brother was still living) could not afford to make him any allowance, but rented to him one of his farms to make what he could out of it. This Lord Mayo farmed himself ("Many a day," he used to say, "have I stood the livelong day in the market selling my beasts,") and made enough out of it to enable him to attend Parliament regularly from after Easter to the end of the Session.

mental way throughout his many years of service in India as a District Officer, and who was fairly conversant with all the then more modern German and English writings on the theory and practice of agriculture.

The Secretary of State remarked (replying as it were officially to what Lord Mayo had written to him on this subject privately or demi-officially) that the next head of the Department was to be chosen for his knowledge of revenue and not of agricultural matters.

It will be seen, therefore, that, as constituted, this Department never was, and never was intended by the Home Government to be, a Department of Agriculture. Lord Mayo hoped to convert it into this, but with his death India lost the warmest, most competent, and, at the same time, most influential advocate for agricultural reform. No change, such as he contemplated, has ever been made in the constitution of the Department, and succeeding administrations have only made the official bonds more rigid, and converted its chief more and more thoroughly into a mere desk-tied Secretary.

A Secretariat is under no circumstances the form of organisation best suited to the promotion of agricultural development. Still even a Secretariat might do much if it possessed three needful adjuncts :

(1.) Competent advisers, not tied to an office, but able to move about, collect and digest the necessary facts, and put schemes before it in a shape in which sound decisions can be arrived at.

(2.) A qualified agency, either of its own, or belonging to administrations subordinate to it, to give effect to its decisions.

(3.) Money to expend in giving effect to these and in experiments, &c.

The Department of Revenue, &c., has *never* had *any one* of these three requisites at its command.

The only person connected with it from first to last who has possessed any knowledge of both the theory and practice of agriculture has been the Secretary, who has had always from eight to ten hours a day (and often much more) office work, and who for ten years has barely seen a field, except from the train, on the occasion of the half-yearly migration of the Government of India between Simla and Calcutta.

It has never had any agency, though the creation of a Directorship of Agriculture in the North-Western Provinces in recent years has at last originated a nucleus in *one* province out of which such an agency will, it is to be hoped, develop. Last, but not least, it has had no money.

How it comes that the Government should have no money to spend on improving the one branch of industry to which it chiefly owes its revenue, will be briefly discussed further on. At present it is sufficient to say that it had *not* the money to give. There was no illiberality. Without a fundamental alteration in its entire policy, no Government, situated as ours has been, could have given for agricultural reform anything that would have been of material use.

Constituted therefore and carried on under these conditions, no one possessing any real insight into what is required could ever have expected from this Department any very tangible results in the way of agricultural reform.

Its possible sphere of action in this direction was limited to a degree that rendered almost nugatory any efforts it might make.

Still it never abandoned the tradition of what its ultimate object was intended to be. What little did fall within its reach it dealt with in the best fashion that its means and appliances permitted.

But what little it may have done (and of this a brief account will be found in the appendix, note B.) is to what is requisite, if any tangible results are to be secured within any reasonable period, as the scratchings of sparrows' feet to deep ploughing.

And the soil we have to deal with is the stiffest of clay: an indigenous agriculture, that no frost of our disapproval will disintegrate; self-coherent from the intermixture of the traditions and superstitions, almost a religion in themselves, of innumerable past ages.

If this Department has succeeded in some solitary instance in doing a minute amount of good in such matters, it is much as though a grain falling by chance into the little bird's tracts, and favoured by unusual fortune, gave rise to a solitary plant boasting some few good ears, and bears to what it ought to have accomplished had it been properly constituted much the same proportion that those straggling ears do to the massive yield of some adjacent well-ploughed field.

What that proper constitution would have been may, perhaps, be gathered by looking back to what Lord Mayo first contemplated; to what he would have carried out had the decision rested entirely with him.

Lord Mayo's original conception of this Department was as a purely agricultural bureau, presided over immediately by a Director-General of Agriculture and not by a Secretary. He considered the subject too great to admit of its being satisfactorily dealt with, unless the best man available gave it his entire time and thoughts. He intended the Director-General to be supreme in his own Department, and only nominally attached for official purposes to one or other Secretariat, in the same way as the Director-General of Post Offices is practically supreme in all departmental matters, though nominally attached to the Financial Department.

The Director-General was to have immediately under him a small staff of experts, and was to keep up only just such an office as was absolutely unavoidable. There was to be as little writing and as much actual work as possible. Directors of Agriculture were to be appointed in each province, also to be aided by experts. They were to work partly through the direct agency of farms* and agricultural schools, and partly through the revenue officials of all grades down to the village accountants. The Director-General was to be

---

* By farms are to be here understood real model farms on carefully selected sites, presided over by picked experts, and liberally supplied with funds and all requisite appurtenances. No plots of waste, such as of late years have almost universally done duty as model farms, waste brought roughly under cultivation by amateurs or florists, who never enjoyed a single day's real training in either theoretical or practical agriculture, and never had at their command more than a fraction of the funds requisite, if justice was to be done to their charges. That these gentlemen and their so-called farms were unsuccessful was surely their misfortune, not their fault, and they deserve, most of them, much credit for doing their best. But let no one gauge the capacity for good, in solving agricultural problems and in imparting agricultural knowledge, of well organized model farms by these failures.

moving about generally whilst the crops were on the ground. He was to confer personally with all the Provincial Directors and their Governments, go thoroughly with the aid of his staff into all their projects and schemes, make himself fully acquainted with local wants and wishes, and then during the hot season join the Government of India, and lay before it as succinctly as possible all that was desired with his (and his experts') opinions and recommendations. He was to watch closely all the schemes and experiments carried out by the Provincial Directors, to furnish them with suggestions, information, and advice; to procure for them, if they wished it, chiefly through the Agricultural Societies of Europe and America, any information, seeds, cattle, sheep, models of implements, &c., that they required; to keep all fully informed through the medium of his journal of what all the rest were doing; and as his experience and practical knowledge increased, and alternate failures and successes gradually indicated these, to lay down the broad lines of the general policy in regard to agricultural matters that the Government should pursue.

In connection with the Provincial Directors were to be model and experimental farms, which were to be at the same time agricultural schools of one grade or another, some of the farms being more specially devoted to the improvement of seed by selection, others to the introduction and acclimatisation of exotic staples, others to the trial of implements and mechanical appliances, others to stock-breeding, others to the purposes of tuition, and so on. Mechanical engineers were to be employed in connection with some of these farms and schools, whose special duty it was to be to adapt the results (where implements of all kinds were concerned) of European and American science, to the wants and means of the Indian husbandman. At first the best civil officers available were to be picked out as Directors, and the best available trained European agriculturists were to be got out to direct the schools and farms, and act as advisers to the Director-General and Directors. Continuity was to be secured by making the service one; Directors were to be promoted to Director-General, experts and heads of farms and schools were to be promoted to Directorships. Gradually, as the expert element acquired knowledge of the country, people, and language, the non-expert element of civilians was to be allowed to disappear. There was to be constituted a compact agricultural service in two divisions, the lower and larger one recruited entirely from the Indian schools, the smaller and higher division recruited to a certain extent from the lower, but, at any rate for many years, mainly from home.

Under the Director-General a Journal of Agriculture was to be issued. A separate and competent editor was to be employed, but the Director-General was to be responsible, and he was to secure for it the aid of all his own and all the Provincial Agricultural Officers. The collection of agricultural statistics was to be the work of the local Directors, but the further tabulation of these statistics, and the preparation from the provincial reports of a monthly or fortnightly summary of the prospects and progress of the crops on the model of those issued by the Bureau at Washington—then, I believe, a new thing—was to be done by the Director-General or his immediate subordinates. The prices in Europe and elsewhere of important articles of Indian produce in which no trade already existed, were to be carefully enquired into by the Director, and published from time to time, and, if necessary, experimental shipment of articles in which a profitable trade seemed probable, undertaken. As the scheme developed itself, Government revenue officials were to be instructed to use their utmost endeavours to lead the landholders of each district to constitute Agricultural Associations; they were to be urged and encouraged to send some of their relatives to the schools. Exhibitions were to be held, prizes given, and every effort made to give dignity in the eyes of the natives to the pursuit of agricultural science. But nothing of this was to be attempted until some distinct success had been achieved which could be pointed to as proof that we had really something to teach, which it would pay to learn.

There were a great many other details, but these do not call for recapitulation here, even were this possible. The above sufficiently indicates the main outlines of Lord Mayo's original scheme.

All experience in other branches of the administration, in Forests, Post Offices, Telegraphs, Education, Surveys, leads irresistibly to the conclusion that Lord Mayo's first idea was the right one, and that until some such distinct and thoroughly homogeneous organisation is here created for this express purpose, no very perceptible or *remunerative* improvement in Indian agriculture can be looked for.

But the present Secretary of this Department, at that time residing with Lord Mayo, and with whom he discussed all the details repeatedly, prepared an estimate, the best he could then furnish, of the cost of carrying out such a scheme, including Director-General and seven Directors, and their staffs and offices, and forty model farms, with schools or colleges of one grade or another attached, contingencies and plant, &c. &c., showing that the *net* expenditure when the scheme was in full play would amount to nearly 25 lakhs of rupees (£250,000) a year, independent of an initial, virtually unreproductive, outlay for offices and buildings of possibly not less than 25 lakhs (£250,000).

Lord Mayo, when convinced that this estimate (avowedly tentative) was in the main not a grossly exaggerated one, considered the whole thing as utterly hopeless, and fixed his mind on carrying a much more modest and admittedly imperfect scheme, to serve as a beginning, a peg to which as time went on all else could be by degrees appended. Even this idea was greatly modified before the scheme was officially put forth; this, again, was met with perhaps the most strenuous opposition any long-considered project of a Viceroy, himself a practical expert in the particular subject, ever encountered, and when at the last the Department was created, it had lost every one of the essential characters on which its possible success as a Bureau of Agriculture was absolutely dependent. It has done, it is hoped and believed, some good and useful work in other branches, but as regards agriculture it was and still remains virtually impotent.

That from the traditional and long-established Indian administrative point of view, Lord Mayo was right in considering the expenditure likely to be involved prohibitive, no experienced Indian official will deny. But the question remains whether from the earliest period of our rule our administration, as regards this most important matter, has not been utterly and fundamentally wrong; whether we have not systematically ignored the gold at our door-steps, while we moved heaven and earth to scrape together copper from all quarters of the globe; whether our present position, as regards local agriculture, after so long a period of rule, is not the very most conspicuous blot on our administration; and whether many of the more serious of our internal troubles, past and present, debt, famine, and discontent, have not been mainly and directly due to the long-continued failure to realise what is alike our duty and our interest, where agriculture is concerned.

Our mighty military expenditure has always been (whatever people unacquainted with the country may think) to a very great extent beyond our control. The exigencies of our position, and the irrepressible growth of our empire, have been such as to render impracticable any great reduction in this item.

But in our civil expenditure, which really was within control, we have, with the best of intentions, misapplied too large a share of the limited funds available.

We have gone on elaborating in every branch highly organised systems of administration which were alike beyond the wants and the wealth of our Indian fellow-subjects.

So long as the masses of the population remained

as poor, and therefore necessarily as ignorant, as they still are, all that was needed was a rough system of patriarchal administration, a purified and somewhat systematised reproduction of the native rule that we replaced, a development of the then existing (now unfortunately almost extinct) system of local self-government by juries, and a rigid repression of all crimes of violence. Under such a form of government, and it has existed for a time in almost every province we have acquired, the people have ever been more contented and better satisfied with their lot than under any of the more advanced and Europeanised forms that have later always displaced it.

Had one-fourth only of what has been expended in developing the existing elaborate and unpopular system of civil administration been steadily and judiciously employed in the improvement of agriculture, had even only the same energy and the same funds been devoted to this purpose, that have been devoted to the cause of education, the people would now be comparatively wealthy, famines would have been greatly limited in area, and their pressure, even within these narrowed limits, greatly lessened, and there would have been no necessity for those unpopular cesses, license taxes, and the like, which, however inevitable, create equally inevitable discontent, and the land revenue of the country, our main source of income, would have stood at at least 30* per cent. above its present level.

---

* If the produce were increased by 50 per cent., we could *double* our land revenue, and yet leave all classes dependent on the land better off than they are now.

Without undervaluing anything that has been done, above all in the direction of education, it can scarcely be denied that the first essential is to fill the stomachs of the people, and that a certain degree of material comfort, considerably in excess of what the masses of the population now enjoy, must be attained before any *real* necessity can exist for elaborate* systems of civil administration. That we have spent our money in these rather than in promoting what would have simultaneously enriched the people and the Government, in a degree that no other conceivable measure could approach, must be held to have been a most grievous error.

That with proper manuring and proper tillage, every acre, broadly speaking, of land in the country can be made to yield 30, 50, 70 per cent. (according

* In a recent debate (7th May 1879) in the Imperial Legislative Council, the Hon. Mr. Cockerell remarked:—

"For an elaborate Code of Procedure naturally not only promoted an increase of litigation, but also tended in a still more marked degree to enhance the time occupied in the disposal of every contested suit. The Secretary to the Government of the North-West Provinces, in a letter addressed to the Government of India relating to this measure, wrote:—

"'*Although Sir George Couper has always been strongly in favour of the non-regulation system, he must admit that, owing to various causes, it is now out of date. It is enough to mention one fact; and that is, the number of legal practitioners who practise in our Courts. Formerly the parties appeared in person, and the Judge had little difficulty in ascertaining the facts of the case. Now, in a great number of suits, the parties are represented by barristers or pleaders; it is not only much more difficult to get at the bottom of the case, but a great deal of time is taken up by the arguments of the lawyers; and it is no exaggeration to say that a case which would formerly have been disposed of in one hour now often occupies the Court for two days.*'"

to circumstances) more of every kind of crop than it at present produces, and this with a fully corresponding increase in the profits of cultivation, is a patent fact that the writer has proved with almost every common North-Western Provinces' crop, that Mr. Robertson has proved with most of the Southern Indian staples, that has been in fact established as well as any point can be, until the masses prove it for themselves.

But—and this is the explanation of the apparent apathy that has ever left our most important source of revenue, the only one capable of very great development, absolutely, if I may use the phrase, uncultivated—the immense majority of officials in India never have, and do not to this day in the least believe it, while the very few who do realise it as an abstract truth, stand aghast at the gigantic nature of the task involved in securing the supply and use of this proper manure and recourse to this proper tillage.

It is, however, just to pick to pieces a formidable obstacle like this, that looms so portentous when viewed from a distance and *en masse*, and to demolish it in detail, that a special and skilled agency is required.

And, whatever the expense involved, it would seem that, looking to the enormous magnitude of the mere pecuniary interests at stake and the almost overwhelming necessities that oppress us, we should, we *must*, have that agency.

After all, a healthy equilibrium of the finances is a primary condition of the well-being of the State. Can anything be more gloomy than *our* financial prospects? More money we must have; *much* more as time goes on; look round on all possible sources of income and say *where* there is any hope of such a material increment as, in the face of an ever-falling exchange, would relieve our anxieties on this score.

From the opium revenue, long threatened, but like threatened men living long, we can at best expect no permanent material increase. Insolvent as we are, an Imperial policy demands the reduction of our customs duties. Stamps and excise might each yield some trifling increment, but the former at a greater cost, perhaps, where the true interests of the people are concerned, than it would be worth. Three or four extra millions might be on a temporary emergency extracted from salt, without much local dissatisfaction, but only in direct opposition to the policy which the Government have so earnestly avowed. Lastly, by additional direct taxation, a couple or even three millions extra might be raised, but not without creating the most widespread discontent that any accident might develop into a costly outbreak or series of outbreaks.

We have really only the land to look to, and here, though we have for generations steadily refused to see it, the gold lies thickly for the gathering.

It is one of those incomprehensible instances of determined national blindness of which history records too many similar examples, but it is a fact that, landlords of an estate, let on comparatively short leases, with a gross rental of seventeen millions,* with the

* I exclude about four and a half millions, the revenue derived from permanently settled and quit-rent estates.

full knowledge that the great mass of our land is yielding less than two-thirds of what it should and would if properly cultivated, we absolutely in practice refuse to take one single material step towards remedying this lamentable waste of our property.

We spend millions on the minds and morals of our fellow-subjects, but shrink, as if from a crime, from spending a quarter of a million on what would bring to each that full quota of daily food they need, and which the masses now never enjoy for any twelve consecutive months, and with this would relieve the State of the existing all over-shadowing financial incubus.*

Here, in improved agriculture, lies the one reasonable hope of extricating ourselves from our difficulties, and our present apparently almost hopeless financial position offers the most irresistible argument against further delay.

So long as things went fairly smooth with us, as we could drift along after a fashion and pay our way, our neglect of this great source of revenue might, looking to the formidable difficulties which undoubtedly surround the question, be only weak and foolish, but

---

* I need scarcely point out that it would not only be directly as regards the food of the people and their land revenue that improved agriculture would operate. Increased production would involve an increase in exports, and *pro tanto* probably some diminution of the exchange burthen. It means an increase of imports, and a relief to manufacturing interests at home, who then might realise (hungry men can rarely stop to be rigidly honest about the food they grasp) the true merits of their recent cry and leave us the remnants of our customs. In a dozen ways, it would act and re-act beneficially.

now, when herein appears to lie our sole hope of renewed prosperity, to hesitate longer would be criminal.

Unfortunately, while none will deny our necessities, few, very few, are competent at this stage to realise the certainty of the ultimate success of the proposed remedy. Of those even who clearly admit the theoretic truth of the proposition, the vast majority will at once recur to innumerable practical difficulties, and if we are not prepared with immediate answers for each, abandon the whole project as impracticable, forgetting that it is just to sift these difficulties, to gather the right facts in regard to, and bring a scientific method of solution to bear upon them, that we in the first instance require the powerful organisation suggested.

The best European experts, selected specially with reference to the peculiar qualifications required for our purposes here, and working hand in hand with the ablest of our Indian Revenue and Irrigation Officers, will unquestionably meet with difficulties at every step; but nothing is more certain than that all such difficulties must disappear when attacked in a thoroughly systematic and scientific method.

No matter how complicated and ill-conditioned the knot, the patient tracing out of each string reveals the point where the first advance may be successfully made, and this done, the next and the next "follow fast and follow faster," till all that once seemed so tangled becomes smooth and straight.

But this absolute certainty of ultimate success, of a success yielding results beyond what the majority would now even dare to *hope* for, is in no degree incompatible with a full realisation of the difficulties that do at present bar its attainment.

No magic transformation can be looked for. With the most careful selections, the utmost energy and good will on the part of all concerned, three or four years must elapse before, with an organisation such as is proposed, the men will have really settled down to their work, and perhaps as many more before all the most important problems, first demanding solution, will have been clearly marked out. Even then it may be only slowly that with silent fingers Science will unpick the knots, and if as, without being in any degree sanguine, we may fairly expect, after twenty years' work, and after spending four or five millions, the main obstacles have been overcome, a thorough reform effected in the agriculture of particular localities, and the people as a whole awakened to what can be and has been done in this way, we shall have made the best investment that ever landed proprietor did.

It will be said that five millions is an enormous sum. But then the return is certain; it may be more or less delayed, but it is the one investment that will, we know, return cent. per cent. and more.

It is as though one were sinking a shaft to a bed of coal, the depth, quality, and extent of which have been ascertained. It may be far to sink, and some very hard beds to cut through, and here tools break, and there new tools have to be specially designed for the particular work, and the water is troublesome, and some of the beds very loose, and so on; it may be a little sooner or a little later, but we go on, neither grudging time nor expense, because we are certain, from our ascertained facts, that when we do get the coal, it will repay us tenfold all we can have possibly expended in reaching it.

It is not, however, as the sole practicable means of materially increasing our revenues and ultimately restoring our finances to a healthy position that energetic action in improving agriculture in India may be insisted on.

On the contrary, not only is this necessary if we desire any large increase of our land revenue, but it is equally so if we desire to avoid a material diminution of this hereafter.

Notwithstanding the enormous additional areas brought under cultivation, notwithstanding our vast irrigation schemes, and our improved and really admirable systems of settlement, our land revenue (excluding Burmah, still almost virgin soil, and making allowances for annexations, such as those of Oudh, the Punjab, &c.) has, if the rise of prices be taken into account, remained stationary, if it has not actually decreased. Yet the agricultural masses (there are more of them, no doubt) are, to say the least, neither wealthier nor better fed, taking the country as a whole, than they were seventy years ago.

The sole explanation is, that the older tilled lands, as a body, yield now lighter crops than they formerly did.

This is what almost every experienced and intelligent cultivator in Upper India will tell you is the fact in regard to all but that little circle of fields skirting each inhabited site, which gets the great bulk of what little manure is available. This, too, might be gathered by comparing what was reckoned in the "Ain Akbari" as a full yield for several descriptions of crops in the Agra, Muttra, Mynpooree, and Etawah districts (in regard to which the Emperor's information must have been accurate), with the known yield in these same localities at the present time.*

But it seems needless to dwell on arguments of this nature, which are always liable to be directly traversed by people who have no real knowledge of the question, which from the complication of factors combining to produce any crop, in any field, in any season, requires not only a multitude of investigations, but their intelligent manipulation by an expert to establish them (and even then carry no conviction to the generality of minds), when we can prove from the nature of things that such *must* be the case.

Owing to a variety of causes, some of which may be touched on in the next section, agriculture in India has become, and becomes daily, more and more what Liebig happily designated a system of spoliation. Deep as the purse may have been, and rich as much of our soil unquestionably was, it is clear that a time

---

* As the result of scores of careful personal experiments carried out in the Allyghur, Mynpooree, and Etawah districts, the writer would state fourteen bushels an acre of wheat to be a high average for good fields, *i.e.* fields with which their cultivators are fairly satisfied; in other words, for the more successful fields, of the best land, which alone is used for wheat. The "Ain Akbari" gives nineteen bushels as an average yield in those days. I need not say how far both these figures fall short of the yield of well-tilled first-class lands, in East Norfolk for instance.

must arrive when, by continually taking out a great deal and putting back very little, both purse and soil are exhausted.

Unlike the European peasant, the Indian husbandman more or less fully realises the evils of this system; it is only on compulsion that he robs his mother soil, and it is only in comparatively quite recent times that this spoliation has acquired the alarming intensity that now characterises it.

Only fifty years ago, when jungles and grazing grounds abounded, when cattle were more numerous, when much wood was available as fuel, there was actually a much greater amount of manure available and a very much smaller number of fields on which to spread it.

The evil is a growing one, it is one of gigantic magnitude, and though, like all great causes, it operates slowly, no one who has really watched agriculture for years in this country can doubt that its effects are already showing far and wide; no one who understands the question can doubt that they will develop with most disastrously increasing virulence as years run on.

Here, again, is a question in regard to which there can be no doubt. How quickly or how slowly a perpetually cropped and rarely, and then only scantily, manured field will become thoroughly exhausted and unculturable, depends, of course, on what we may term the original capital of that field, and on the proportion that may exist between the disbursements and receipts, but it being admitted that the former are and have been for years greatly in excess of the latter, and that this disproportion is increasing, the ultimate result is certain.

That the gradual (and perhaps later suddenly rapid) deterioration of the major portion of our cultivated lands is, unless a totally new system be inaugurated, inevitably impending, can be denied by no one conversant with the subject.

It is impossible for Government to disbelieve this; they may think, and perhaps rightly, that it will last their time, but they cannot doubt as to what they are preparing for their successors.

And it is not as in other countries, where the land is private property. It is its own land that Government is allowing to go to ruin, its own financial blood that it lets run to waste. This is the sole goose that ever would or could lay golden eggs for us, and we are smiling as it is slowly starved before us, and will not make a single effort worthy of the name to arrest the catastrophe.

Yet again, from another and distinct source, ruin and desolation, more palpable and speedy in its course, though more limited in its operation, await vast tracts in Northern India, unless the voice of reason can gain a hearing and science be allowed to guide agriculture.

In Oudh, the Panjab, and the North-West Provinces, the soils mostly contain an appreciable admixture of saline particles. With the construction of high-level canals, the subsoil water level is raised, the surface flooded, the earth yields up its soluble salts to the water, which again restores them (but on the surface) as it passes away in vapour. At first the result may be good, and marvellous are the crops that have been raised in the Doab on the first introduction of canal irrigation, owing to the first slender doses of potash and chloride of sodium.

But nature works on blindly and unceasingly. The water below searches out one by one each soluble particle in excess of the particular soil's capacity of retention, and, as it slowly creeps up by capillary attraction, leaves these ever behind it on the surface.

Time passes on, some crops begin to be unprofitable; in the hottest time of the year, a glimmer as though of a hoar frost overspreads the land. The land grows worse and worse, but ever night and day nature works slowly on, and the time comes when, abandoned by the cultivator, the land glitters white and waste as though thickly strewn with crisp, new-fallen snow; never, alas! to melt away, except under the rays of science.

Along the little old Western Jumna Canal, thousands of fields are to be seen thus sterilised. Along the course of the mighty Ganges Canal—a work as it were but of yesterday—the dreary wintry-looking rime is already in many places creeping over the soil.

Come it quickly or come it slowly, the ultimate result here also is certain; and, unless a radical change is effected in existing arrangements, we know, as definitely as we know that the sun will rise to-morrow, that the time must come when some of the richest arable tracts in Northern India will have become howling saline deserts.

The task, no doubt, looked at from a distance, seems almost a hopeless one, but when it is more closely examined, and when we fully realise the vast strength of our revenue and irrigation establishments throughout all those portions of the empire in which we have the most direct interest in the progress of agriculture,* it will be perceived that the plant for much of the work is already on the ground, and that all that is primarily necessary is an efficient directing and controlling agency.

III.

Some of the problems that would at the outset engage the attention of an Indian Bureau of Agriculture.

Assuming that now, *at last*, some real steps will be taken in the direction of agricultural reform, it may be useful to glance at some few of those problems which should apparently at the outset engage the attention of any working department of agriculture in India.†

---

* In Lower Bengal no doubt these establishments are weak, but then the land revenue is here permanently settled, and we have not the same *immediate* pecuniary interest in the reform of agriculture there.

† I have no doubt that many will be inclined to urge that Agricultural education—a kind of education infinitely more needed than the education in Law and Letters, now given at such a vast cost in our Colleges and Universities—is one of the first things to be undertaken, and that Agricultural manuals and text-books, with object lessons in elementary schools, &c., are primary essentials.

But this is not my view—these things, good as they are, belong to a more advanced stage of progress.

At the outset, the Agricultural Department will have mainly to teach itself. Scientific truths are immutable, but their profitable

First and foremost unquestionably stands the increased provision of manure, not merely because this is the crying want of Indian agriculture, but because unavoidably any practicable arrangement for supplying this want must at the same time supply many other minor ones.

We may pass lightly over the first branch of this subject, viz. the introduction of the Chinese system, because though by the help of combined tact and authority, kindness, patience, and gentle pressure, it *could* even now be introduced, in two or three years, into *any* small, well-supervised tract, and thence spread gradually over the entire empire, every one conversant with agricultural literature knows all about it, and knows that it would in India need for its support legislation, and a happy combination of enthusiasm and discretion in working the law, that at the present time is scarcely to be expected.

---

application demands a thorough knowledge of the entire environment of the particular position, a thorough comprehension of local conditions, and we cannot usefully begin to teach natives the theory of Agriculture until we have first taught ourselves (and are, therefore, in a position to teach them also) how, under the peculiar local conditions, of India and different provinces of India, we can advantageously give practical effect to that theory.

I may add, though this is a distinct but germane question, that I believe in teaching botany, vegetable physiology, chemistry, and geology in schools, and practical farming on a farm; I do not advocate mixing up the two. For the great mass a practical training and the enforcement, as axiomatic rules of action, of certain definite maxims and precepts, is all-sufficient. To the few whose capacities are of a higher order, or whom circumstances call to a higher position, a thorough scientific education should be first given, and then they should, in a distinct institution, be initiated in the full practice of what they have already mastered in theory.

Undoubtedly the introduction of this system which, while hugely benefiting agriculture, would perhaps do more than any other conceivable measure to restrict the ravages of cholera, should never be lost sight of. Its importance cannot be over-rated, but the immediate difficulties to be encountered, and the prejudices to be overcome, are (or *seem* to be, for this may be *partly* a chimera) so great that action in this direction may reasonably be postponed while there is so much else immediately practicable to be done.

Setting this aside, the main causes of the scarcity of manure are the comparative paucity of cattle, and the almost universal use of their dung as fuel.

The paucity of cattle is due almost entirely to the incredible losses of stock sustained from starvation and different forms of cattle disease. The consumption of their droppings as fuel is due to the impossibility, in some places, or expense, in others, of procuring wood.

Over a great portion of the empire, the mass of the cattle are starved for six weeks every year. The hot winds roar, every green thing has disappeared, no hot-weather forage is grown, the last year's fodder has generally been consumed in keeping the well bullocks on their legs during the irrigation of the spring crops, and all the husbandman can do is just to keep his poor brutes alive on the chopped leaves of the few trees and shrubs he has access to, the roots of grass and herbs that he digs out of the edges of fields, and the like.

In good years he just succeeds; in bad years, the weakly ones die of starvation. But then come the rains. Within the week, as though by magic, the burning sands are carpeted with rank luscious herbage, the cattle *will* eat and over-eat, and *millions* die of one form or other of cattle disease, springing out of this starvation, followed by sudden repletion with rank, juicy, immature herbage.

Many years ago, the writer, when advocating the establishment of Veterinary Colleges,* estimated the

---

* I quote from the memorandum on this subject which I submitted to Government:—

"According to censuses taken in the Punjab, Central Provinces, &c., there is at present in India about one head of horned cattle to every two human beings. This would give us about 100 millions of cattle, worth at the very lowest calculation £75,000,000."

* * * * * * *

"It is not too much to say that one-half the whole capitalised wealth of ninety-nine hundredths of the whole population of India is to be found in their cattle; it is not too much, I believe, to assume that the value of this cattle falls little, if at all, short of 75 millions sterling. Hitherto diseases of the most virulent character have raged amidst agricultural stock unchecked, and almost unknown to and uncared for by the Government. Periodically, plagues and murrains have devastated vast districts, sweeping away the hard-earned savings of millions, and not only depriving them of the means of subsistence, but seriously endangering the food supply of the empire. Are we to accept such calamitous visitations as dispensations of Providence to be acquiesced in humbly, and submitted to as inevitable? The spirit of the present age will permit no such passive submission. Misfortune and disease will and must come; but whether in the case of man or beast, it is for intelligent rulers to struggle against the calamity, and circumscribe, by every effort that science can suggest, the limits of its action. Everything must have a commencement. Sanitation of human beings has been set on foot, and we have now that of their humble but indispensable servants to care for. I expect no great success at first. I look for no *immediately* valuable results. The best trees take longest to grow. All I ask is to be allowed to plant the seed; and I submit that, having regard to the circumstances of the country, it is no unreasonable average annual loss of cattle in India by preventible cattle disease of one form and another, at fully ten million beasts, roughly valued at £7,500,000, and subsequent experience and enquiry has led him to believe that this estimate materially understated the case.

The Indian climates, varying as these do, appear to be specially favourable to cattle. Every one who has kept cattle here knows that if moderately fed, and given plenty of work and kept away from contagion, they never seem to be sick or sorry, but work on, hardy and healthy, from youth to extreme old age. They are very prolific too. If our poor beasts only had reasonably fair play, the whole empire would swarm with cattle, and cattle able to work the heaviest ploughs, and, in soils and situations where this was necessary or desirable, to plough as deep as you like.

---

request to urge a grant of £1,000, and a yearly allowance (for the present) of about half that sum, to secure the establishment of an institution, which, if a success, will pave the way to an efficient system for bringing cattle epidemics by degrees more and more under control, and for introducing throughout the Bengal Presidency improved methods of dealing with stock, both in health and in disease."

This project received Lord Mayo's warmest support; it was, in fact, his own idea worked out by the writer. Before the design could be carried out he was taken from us. His successor promised support. The principal of the first College was nominated, the premises even were taken, and the necessary alterations in them commenced, when the then Viceroy changed his mind, started off the Principal, Mr. J. B. Hallen (*the only* man then in India who could have successfully inaugurated this important work) elsewhere, and "concluded" the project. *Ex uno disce omnes!*

But what can be expected under existing conditions? Annually a rigid Lent, too often merging into actual starvation, followed by a sudden gorging with unwholesome food. The people are keenly alive to the dangers of such alternations, and labour hard to prevent the latter, or they would not keep a single head alive; but despite all their care, their losses are enormous. In bad years, whole provinces are devastated. But a few years ago more than half the cattle in Oudh were lost during two successive bad seasons.

And be it noted that it is not only the supply of manure that this fearful mortality amongst the cattle, and their resulting paucity, so greatly restricts; it is the little hoarded capital of the peasant, the very mainspring of agriculture in India, that is thus flung away. There is nothing new in all this; everybody in India, Government and people, all know it, after a fashion, but beyond putting a single veterinary surgeon in a couple of provinces to try and train a score of native cow doctors, nothing is done. Nothing ever will be done until there is a special and properly organised department, whose sole business it is to look after it.

Some are cautious: "We must begin gradually," say they; "Rome was not built in a day," &c. Every one knows these nauseating commonplaces by rote.

Well and good, they make their infinitesimally minute beginning, but the moment you desire to go on, there is the cry of expense, "We cannot afford it."

The policy of the Government of India in these matters for the last twenty-five years can only be likened to that of some nobleman, who, with his magnificent palace slowly burning beneath his gaze, first, after much hesitation, allows you to hire a boy with a penny squirt, as a beginning, to prove that water *can* extinguish fire, and then, this simple fact established, directly you urge the hire of a powerful steam fire-engine to take up the work of extinction in earnest, shudders at the expense and will hear nothing further on the subject.

But to return : Prevention is better than cure, and desirable, nay essential, as it will become later to disseminate correct veterinary knowledge amongst Indian agriculturists, and place sound advice on all matters connected with the treatment of cattle in health as well as in disease, within every villager's reach, the first thing clearly is to attack the root of the evil and to mitigate the intensity of those causes to which three-fourths of the mortality amongst Indian cattle are primarily due.

It is the hot-weather privations that have first to be dealt with.

Now, no doubt, it may seem easy to deal with this. European agriculturists will say, "What simpler? Grow sorgho, Guinea grass, &c. &c.," and probably twenty years hence, when the Agricultural Department gets a real hold upon the country and the people, and other changes to be hereafter foreshadowed have come about, this *will* be done to a certain extent. But at present the condition of the people is such that it is doubtful whether even the most stringent legislation, worked by the most energetic executive, would secure any such general growth of hot-weather forage as would, taking the country as a whole, materially ameliorate the miserable lot of our cattle.

Fairly good land, and a great deal of it, would be wanted, and the people can't spare this; and irrigation is essential, and this is not at all generally available during the hot weather; and a certain amount of capital would be required, and the people have it not; and the money-lenders would not advance it for a crop of which the greater part was not to come to them direct, *and* it is altogether a *new* thing, such as neither they nor their fore-fathers ever heard of; and, though in particular localities it might from the very outset be pressed, and perhaps successfully, on some few of the people, it must be many many years before there can be the smallest chance of its general adoption.

But there is one thing that can be done—a thing that is entirely in accord with the traditions of the country—a thing that the people would understand, appreciate, and, with a little judicious pressure, co-operate in, and that is the planting up with trees of a certain sufficient area in *every* village in the drier portions of the country.

The undertaking is a very large one, but presents no insuperable difficulties; it is a gigantic hill to cut away, but it is all earth and no rock, its greatness is purely numerical. There are an immense number of spadesful to be lifted, but the lifting each is perfectly easy. Energy, perseverance, and time are all that is necessary. Once a sufficient area planted in each neighbourhood as a communal forest, and the cattle difficulty is at an end; the forest would be closed till other fodder was consumed and the fields were bare, and then they would be opened to the village herds. In India, wherever you have a closed grove of trees, there spontaneously you have a luxuriant growth of herbage, and at the end of April, even in the hottest and driest parts of Upper India, where the whole country round is as bare as any desert, you will find in preserved groves (such as the more wealthy zemindars often keep for their own cattle and in view to the sale of the grass in neighbouring towns) a mass of hay above and green grass below, that is perfectly astounding.

This is due partly to the rich humus, the result of the decay for many years of fallen twigs and leaves, and partly to the diminished evaporation from the soil protected by the trees.

But with this improved provision of fodder we obtain simultaneously an improved supply of fuel, and an immediate great diminution in the consumption of manure as such. Very few natives will cook with cow-dung cakes if they can procure sticks, and it is chiefly for cooking* purposes that fuel is required in India. Moreover, in the wood ashes we have a new useful source of manure.

Two main questions would have to be considered :—First, how the land is to be obtained; second, how it is to be planted.

For the first, legislation would be required. Recourse to the Act would not be necessary in all cases;

---

* Doubtless *chiefly* for cooking, but there is a vast consumption in brick-making, and here the P. W. D. are great sinners. The increase of brick-making, and with it, the consumption of dung as fuel (it being, in most places, cheaper than wood), has been enormous of late years.

a great deal could be done by the influence of the local officials, but the power to act with or without consent must be taken.

In some places, Government has plenty of land of its own which it could plant up, but this is almost exclusively in thinly populated and imperfectly settled tracts where no special action is required. Generally throughout those portions of the empire where this planting up is most urgently required, the Government has little or no land in its own exclusive possession. It is a sleeping partner in *all* the land, but it has made the management over to landholders of one class or another, whom it has taken in as working partners, on condition of receiving certain yearly payments, supposed to be equivalent to half the average profits. Such payments are fixed for longer or shorter periods, and are liable to alteration at the close of these at the pleasure of the Government.

In almost every village, larger or smaller tracts of land are to be found quite good enough for planting up with hardy trees, but yet too poor to be worth cultivating; while besides these there are often considerable tracts of land, which, though culturable, are never cultivated, and bring in nothing to the landholder. Legal authority would be required to set apart portions or the whole* of such lands as com-

* Under any circumstances, as this land serves, after a fashion, as a grazing ground, it could rarely be taken up *at once* as a whole. Part would be first planted, and five or six years later, when the trees in that part were sufficiently large to allow of the admission of cattle, another part would be taken up, and so on.

munal forests, without any compensation to the landholder, *unless* it appeared that he derived any revenue therefrom, and that in consequence of the action thus taken, his receipts from his estate (technically called the "assets") were reduced below twice the Government rent, or as we call it, revenue.

In nine cases out of ten no compensation would be required, and certainly at first I would only attempt to deal with the nine cases and leave the tenth, in which compensation would be necessary, to stand over till the people had fully realised the enormous advantages of the scheme.

At the first glance it may be thought that what is proposed would involve a serious and indefensible interference with the rights of private property. It may be said: "True, these landholders are not absolute proprietors in the sense that we understand the word in England; their tenures are more like copyholds, subject to periodical enhancement of rents at the will and pleasure of the real proprietor, the State, but still they have a certain proprietary right, which they can in most places sell and mortgage and bequeath, a right to continue to hold the land undisturbed, so long as they continue to pay the demand which the State from time to time assesses on it."

Clearly we could not take any thing that directly helps them to pay this assessment, without a corresponding diminution in this latter; but our primary condition is, that we shall grant this, where this is equitably required, and that we shall at first confine our action to lands which are at present bringing in nothing. And we are not going to take these lands away, nor are we going to derive any direct benefit from them. We are going to convert land, now valueless, into land which will directly and indirectly enrich alike landholder and cultivators; we, in fact, only re-assume control over certain lands (in which, be it remembered, we are partners) because their utilisation in the manner demanded by our interests, the landholders' interests, and the interests of the entire nation, requires an organisation and intelligence that our managing partners cannot command and do not possess.

Looking to all that depends upon the measure, looking to the impossibility of carrying it out without State interference, I do not think that the most ardent advocate for non-interference with private rights would deny that here was a case in which it was not only justifiable, but incumbent, on the State to interfere.

I do not go further into details; every one's ideas on such a subject must be crude until we actually begin to carry out the work in practice. It is to elaborate the practical details of procedure here as in other matters that we require a special organisation.

The land available, it will be necessary to surround it with a good stout mud fence, such as the people now construct around any grove they plant, and the ground inside must be more or less ploughed or broken up, and if the soil be such as to warrant the planting of fruit-trees, such as mangoes, some sort of a well may have to be dug.

I do not hesitate to say that all this the villagers

should be required to do, and that power should be taken to order this, and to punish by some trivial fine disobedience of such orders.

This power existing in the background, no competent revenue officer would find the least difficulty in getting all that was necessary done with the entire good will of the people, and at really no cost to them or the State. There are several periods in the year when every cultivator can give half a day's labour daily at no loss to himself, and when, if not helping at the communal enclosure, he would be idling.

And there are no people in the world that can be more easily led by an intelligent superior into combining to carry out a single work (the benefit of which they understand) under his eye; a few turbans given away and a few sweetmeats would convert the entire business into a sort of festival. Here once let it be clearly understood that the enclosure would be preserved during the cold season, and (after the first five years) thrown open to cattle in the hot season, and every man will appreciate and approve them.

In Mhairwarra, for forest purposes, Government took up *large* reserves. The measure, though necessary, was a very unpopular one. Last year when the country suffered from drought, and the starvation of their cattle stared the people in the face, these reserves were thrown open to them. Forest conservancy was a little thrown back, but the people are no longer opposed to it; on the contrary, they quite appreciate it.

As to *what* should be planted, hardy indigenous trees merely for shade, trees furnishing fruits for men or cattle, in what localities and in what proportions—these are points to be worked out gradually by the Department.

Again, rules will be required to regulate the use and prevent the abuse of these communal forests or groves. A system of management will have to be elaborated, the leading idea of which must be to induce the people to act to the greatest possible extent for themselves. A dozen other details will have to be dealt with, but there is not one single difficulty to be encountered of which we shall not be able to say *solvitur eundo.*

I am quite sure that, looking at the work sketched out, many able and experienced officers will say at first, "It is too vast, it cannot be done." But these same officers would not deny that they could, if vested with the powers above contemplated, make all necessary arrangements and carry out the scheme in, say, a dozen villages. Nor, again, that having done this, they could repeat the operation more readily in another group of hamlets; nor that when thus far advanced, their senior native revenue officers could carry on the work on the same lines in many villages, though some would still require their personal intervention to overcome difficulties. Nor would they deny that one pergunnah completed, the neighbouring ones would be much more easily dealt with, and so on. The truth is the fagot, taken in the lump, *is* rather alarming, but the sticks are all very little, and you have only to pick the fagot to pieces, to make the task a very easy, although a tedious and lengthy, one.

Of course works like these are not to be commenced

broadcast or at random. The work would be begun in specially selected localities, and the greatest available strength turned on to these from Revenue, Irrigation, Forest, and Agricultural Departments; and you would begin prudently, not forcing the measure down any one's throat, but talking about it to everyone, and having public meetings (and very effective these are in the interior of districts if you manage properly) and devoting special endeavours to convincing men who, you know, carry weight locally, and letting it leak out that there will be turbans and dresses of honour for people who materially aid the progress of the scheme, and just possibly a C.S.I. or C.I.E. for any one who carried a large tract of country, and so on. Every one who has carried a new great measure through a district, such as the voluntary 1 per cent. subscription to schools was in the old days, knows all about it, and knows that any harmless and beneficial measure, not opposed to the religious opinions of the people, can be carried by patience, perseverance, and tact, if only it be known that the Government approves, and really wishes, and sooner or later intends, to have it carried.

It may here be noticed that this extensive reboisement, while operating to augment materially the manure supply, to improve the breed and increase the supply of cattle and economise the agricultural capital of the country, cannot fail to exercise a powerful check over the ravages of famine.

How far the increase of trees in level country operates (if at all) to increase the rainfall, is still an open question; but that a tract thickly studded with forests and groves retains the water it receives a great deal longer than one devoid of these, is a matter of every-day experience; and it is certain that widespread and entire failure of crops over enormous areas, such as we have witnessed so often in the last quarter of a century, would have been impossible had cultivation and forest been interlaced throughout them as has been above proposed. There would, no doubt, have been some total failure, and much partial failure, but the intensity of the calamity would, beyond all question, have been much mitigated, and it is quite an open question whether, in some cases, it would not have been altogether averted.

Moreover, it is fair to presume that a considerable proportion of the trees planted will be fruit-trees, the mango for instance, which always fruits most heavily in seasons of drought, and which furnishes a very important, and not unwholesome, supply of food to the people, at the most critical period of years of scarcity.

The enormous increase in the supply of such food that the proposed measure involves would most materially assist the people in tiding over bad seasons on greatly diminished rations of grain.

And in famines, the death of the cattle is almost as disastrous to the State, from a mere utilitarian point of view, as the death of the men, and for the cattle our forests will provide. The cattle will never starve with these wide plantations everywhere, as there are scores of indigenous trees whose foliage furnishes fairly nutritious fodder, and in seasons of great drought the people would be allowed to make the utmost of every leaf.

In many of the tracts where famine has raged, a thorough reboisement, with improvement in cattle, and an abundant supply of manure would admit of deep ploughing, such that, with a large portion of the surface protected by trees, no total failure of the crops *could* result from the failure of a single monsoon.

It is needless, however, to pursue the subject into all its details; my object merely is to convey some general conception of the scheme which, the more it is considered, the more pregnant it will prove of direct and indirect benefits to agriculture in India.

Although all that has been urged in regard to wholesale reboisement is applicable to, perhaps, the major portion of the temporarily settled districts, no one rule holds good, and no one scheme can suffice for the whole of this vast empire. There are regions as large as the British Isles, where no reboisement is requisite, and where altogether different arrangements in regard to supply of manure are needed, where we have chiefly to teach the people more care in collecting it, more care in storing it, resort to available mineral manures, of the value of which they have little or no conception, and the like.

Again, farm-yard manure, though I have laid so much stress on it, as it really contains *everything* that we take out of the land, is not the only organic manure readily available to which the Agricultural Department will have to direct attention. Outside each village is a golgotha, where the bones of all cattle and animals that die whiten and slowly decay in ghastly piles. At present this enormous supply of phosphates is absolutely wasted. Really portable bone-crushers, that could move easily over the sandy village tracks, will have to be devised. These will have to be sent round from village to village, crushing for each community their, at present, useless heaps. The people will have to be taught how, when, in what doses, and for what crops, to administer this powerful fertiliser, and how to increase the rapidity of its action by treating it with sulphuric acid, which latter will have to be *loaned* to them as an advance.

There are districts where it will probably be found necessary to manufacture manures outright, and *advance* them to the cultivators, as any other advance is made, until, their pecuniary value established and a permanent demand created, private enterprise steps in to supply it.

And of course careful analyses of soils (which in India are wonderfully homogeneous over wide areas) would be necessary to indicate with precision the nature of the plant food more especially wanting in each case, whether with reference to a particular soil or a particular crop; but these are among the necessities of scientific agriculture everywhere; there is nothing in regard to them peculiar to India; and, with many other similar matters, they need no special notice here.

Although with diminished mortality and improved condition of cattle, the agricultural capital of the country will be, as time runs on, notably increased, it would be idle to suppose that the generally impoverished condition of the actual cultivators of the soil, almost throughout the empire, will need no other or direct relief.

Wherever we turn we find agriculturists burdened with debts running on at enormous rates of interest. In some districts, even provinces, the evil is all-absorbing—a whole population of paupers, hopelessly meshed in the webs of usurers.

No one probably needs to be told that no farmer or cultivator, hopelessly in debt, can ever do any justice to himself or his land.

If only on account of our own direct and vital interest in the land, some action is necessary on our parts to limit the progress of and gradually wholly eradicate this plague of indebtedness; certainly next to the manure question, there is no other that will earlier demand the attention of the Agricultural Department.

The subject is so large and complicated, its difficulties so protean, and the remedies required necessarily so liable to vary in relation to each of the almost innumerable combinations of circumstances under which the evil will have to be dealt with, that it is impossible to discuss it at all exhaustively in a sketch like this. Still some indication may be given of the manner in which this indebtedness has come about and of the direction in which a remedy for it should be sought.

A theory is at times gravely maintained, even in India, that the ryot is a thriftless, reckless fellow; that no matter what he gets, he will always spend more than his income; that it matters nothing whether the rent he has to pay is high or low; that he rather likes than otherwise having a balance *against* him at his banker's; and that do what one will, he *will* always be in debt.

Nothing can convey a more thoroughly and utterly false conception of our agriculturists as a body.

That these, in common with the entire population, high and low, do, in accordance with immemorial custom,* spend a great deal more upon marriages than according to *English* ideas any similarly circumstanced sane man ought to or would, may be at once admitted.

Any real, vigorous, and persistent action† to check this common form of extravagance, taken under sound native advice, would be a real blessing to the country. But, after all, this is the poor fellow's only extravagance; these are almost the only white days in his dull-coloured life of toil and pinching, and unless he is singularly blessed (or unblest?) there are not many of them, and for the rest, a more careful frugal being is not to be found on earth.

He hates debt; he hates the usurer's name; let any stroke of luck befal him, and see how soon the monstrous account against him is settled. This is not the case merely with individuals, the population of

---

* In most parts of India custom is still, be it remembered, where social matters are concerned, an iron, all-embracing, law.

† Hitherto, as in most other matters in India, there has been a vast amount of "cry," and the smallest possible amount of "wool." Every now and then the question crops up, a great deal of talk ensues, nothing effective is *done*, and the matter drops.

whole provinces (like Guzerat and Berar, owing to the abnormal profits from cotton during the American war) have similarly cleared themselves.

Fools are scarce nowhere, but only show our ryots how to free themselves from the toils of the money-lender and how to keep out of his books, and none need fear that the great mass of them will long remain plunged in their present comparative misery; for misery of a kind it is.

A very happy natured, contented race, as a whole, are our village husbandmen, and they have their little amusements and festivals, and when harvests are very good, pretty much all that, with their simple habits, they need. The picture is not all black, or how could we or any one hold the country? But withal their lives are *very* hard and toilsome, and through it all too many are pressed with debt. Good crops ease the pain a little, and the village merry-making brings a temporary forgetfulness, but the sore is always there, and except in very good seasons multitudes for months in every year cannot get sufficient food for themselves and their families. They are not starving, but they are hungry, they get less than they want and than they ought to have.

No doubt they make the best of it, and keep cheerful under pressure that would crush men of more advanced races, but this very child-like nature involves dangers, and we may see from the Deccan riots and sporadic cases occurring constantly everywhere, that quite independent of the necessities of agricultural reform, and quite apart from the duty of ameliorating a lot on the whole so unenviable, cogent political reasons exist for grappling with this growing evil of indebtedness.

Much has been said about tenures in connection with this matter, and many have ascribed the origin of the present depressed condition of the peasantry to mistakes perpetrated in regard to these.

No doubt many errors have been here committed, and no doubt, other things being as they are, these have powerfully contributed to bring about the present lamentable state of affairs. But the root of the evil is not here, and but for other and utterly distinct mistakes, these errors, though involving in some cases injustice or hardship to individuals, would have brought about no general indebtedness of the agricultural classes.

It has already been remarked that we have wasted on an elaborate, cumbrous, and unsuitable system of civil jurisprudence, money that ought to have been employed in improving our agriculture and increasing the material comforts of the masses; it may now be added that the system on which it was expended has been the chief and direct cause of the major portion of the indebtedness and impoverishment of our agriculturists.

Errors as to tenures; forcing proprietary rights upon people incapable of appreciating or understanding them; forcing upon districts where one system of landholding was indigenous a wholly different, exotic, and therefore unsuitable one; the want of elasticity in our system of realising the revenue; unlimited subdivision of holdings, and a dozen other causes, may be indicated as having, *our courts being as they are,* contributed to it, but these courts themselves are the *fons et origo* of the evil, and had they been the simple summary courts of equity and not of law, which was all the state of the country demanded, all these other causes would have smouldered on almost innocuously.

It is necessary to realise the radical changes that our courts and revenue systems combined have wrought in the position of our agriculturists.

Previous to our rule no private person had, broadly speaking, any property in the soil.* All proprietary right, in the sense in which we at home understand the word, vested directly in the State or vicariously in some powerful chief or official. All that the people as a body enjoyed were a high class of occupancy rights, heritable but not transferable.

A man might be ever so much in debt, but you could not interfere with the land he held, for that was not his, but his ruler's; and such rights as he possessed therein were personal to himself and family, or, in some cases, clan; and if any outsider had obtained possession, the State would have stepped in and resumed the property. No doubt, if sufficiently bribed, the local officials would, and often did, wink at transfers, but these were opposed alike to custom and tradition which then constituted the law, such as it was, on this subject.

There was, therefore, in those days no great in-

---

* We must perhaps except lands given to Brahmins, saints, &c. for temple, mosque, or other religious or charitable purposes; but even these were, properly speaking, inalienable.

ducement to money-lenders to advance money to landholders or cultivators of any degree, still less was it their interest to tempt those to take money, which they really did not want, in order to make an extra display at a wedding or a durbar.

They lent money, but only at enormous rates of interest; but this was not unfair, as they never hoped even to recover the principal, while for such interest as they were to get (a widely different thing to what was written in the bond) they were dependent on the good will of their debtor, or the rare, paternal interference of some superior, who, appealed to with suitable presents, would say, "Come, Rambuksh, you owe the Sahoo Sahib a lot of money, and you have paid him nothing for two years; you just satisfy him by some proper payment on account, or it will not be well for you."

And even such interference was rarely needed, for the people are naturally very honest; the creditor had no object in cheating, because he could, as a rule, only expect to get what he could convince his debtor was justly due, while as for the debtor, though he had no intention of paying off his creditor, whose debt was perhaps six generations old, and who moreover never expected this, still neither had he any objection to make, from year to year, such payments on account as he could afford and as according to custom (everything was custom in those days) were fair and right.

It was a point of honour with him, and the natives of India had a very keen sense of honour; they saw many things from a different point of view to what we do, but they kept, I think, as a whole, closer to their standard than we as a nation have ever kept to ours.

It was almost a point of honour with them to defraud the State, to make false statements to superiors, &c., just as it used to be for boys to rob their master's garden, and mislead him whenever possible; but it would have been as base in their eyes to cheat or bilk their friend, the family banker, as it would have been for the schoolboy to steal from one of his own companions.

So there was debt in those days too, but it hurt nobody; the banker got his annuity so long as things went well, and even if in bad times he got little or nothing, he knew that there were always strong arms and sharp swords, ready to defend him if things went wrong with *him;* each party was dependent more or less on the good offices of the other, and so far from being enemies they were friends, bound together by the remembrance of many acts of mutual kindness, and if by chance they could not agree,—and men, though both honest and well meaning, will at times fall out and differ,—they called in a party of respectable neighbours and friends (whose intervention only cost a good dinner) who heard all both had to say, effected a wise compromise, and settled the matter. There was no appeal; the brotherhood, or mixed jury, as the case might be, had spoken and the matter was at an end.

But with the enlightened rule of the British Government all this was to cease. Brimful of philanthropy, we could not let well alone, or indeed believe that anything could be well for others, which was not in accordance with what we thought good for ourselves. With our innovations, our exotic systems of land and law, we have dissolved the bonds of society, we have turned peace into war, we have arrayed every class against that on which it was most dependent, capitalists against landholders, landlords against tenants, every man almost against his fellow.

There is not, I believe, a single wise and good native of India who will not freely admit that, whatever the failings and shortcomings of individual officers, the motives and intentions of the British Government, where India is concerned, have, on the whole, been pure and noble. But I fear that there is not one who would not condemn, in terms stronger than I have the heart to use, the cruel blunders into which our narrow-minded, though wholly benevolent, desire to reproduce England in India has led us.

We began by conferring proprietary rights (the poor people, no ownership in the soil, mere serfs!) or, where as in Bombay we stopped short of this, we gave additional strength to occupancy rights, and made these transferable. Every one knows the European arguments about enhancing the value of rights by making them transferable. Such a great thing to enable them to be brought into the market! Buying and selling, as a wise writer once said, is an Englishman's idea of Paradise, and in the most unselfish spirit we desired to introduce our native fellow-subjects into this same Paradise.

No one saw that the people were on the whole happy and contented as they were, that their past sufferings, where they had suffered, were due not to any defects in their position or rights as established by custom, but to those rights having been ignored, and that custom having been over-ridden.

No one seems to have realised that the tenures of a country are the outcome of its whole past history, ever, as time rolled on, adjusting themselves to the varying conditions and relations of the different classes of the community. That they must necessarily, therefore, be under the circumstances, those best suited to the country ; that though they may require change as these conditions and relations vary, it must be

> "Change that broadens slowly down from precedent to
> precedent,"

and that any sudden and arbitrary, externally imposed, change must, however noble the impulse that prompted it, involve new and necessarily unsuitable combinations.

Human institutions to be healthy must grow where they are to stand.

Not so reasoned our predecessors. They gave a new value to the land, by rigidly limiting their demand on the soil—a good thing, quite in accordance with the people's ideas of what a good prince should do,—and they conferred partial proprietary rights (which no one wanted or appreciated) wholesale, and they made all the rights they created or acknowledged in the soil transferable.

Up to our time such rights as existed were entailed in the strictest fashion; creditors could not get hold of the land, even during the lifetime of the debtor.

We raised the character of the rights, but cut off the entail without the consent of the heirs.

At first this did no great harm. Nobody understood the change, our people then were no lawyers, courts were few, and administered simple justice according to equity and good conscience, and the majority of civil disputes continued to be settled by the people amongst themselves in the old fashion.

But as times passed on new and new laws were continually made, and courts were multiplied and gradually modified into courts of law, where justice sat fettered by codes, and whence equity and good conscience had been banished for contempt of court, and a swarm of professional pleaders (good and bad, but specially the latter) spread over the length and breadth of the land, and village verdicts ceased to carry weight, and in the simplest matter, which formerly would have been settled on his own village platform by his own brethren and elders, and rightly settled in an hour, a man now had to put up with wrong, or walk twenty miles to court, and fee pleaders, and waste a week or more, and many weeks' earnings, and all as often as not merely to see the wrong triumph. Or, if successful, to be dragged yet another fifty miles, on appeal to a higher court, where there were even more expensive pleaders to fee, and more time and money to waste, dangling about the court-house steps or compound, dogged by peons and emissaries of the underpaid native subordinate officials, all threatening loss of his case, unless he bribed, bribed, bribed. And if he, —*O fortunatus nimium,*—gained his case here too, and prepared to start for his neglected fields, a half-ruined and yet partly happy man, (for natives acquire a passion for litigation, just as Europeans do for drink or gambling,) lo and behold, a second or special appeal on some miserable quibble of law, evolved out of clumsily drawn statutes, and he is dragged away yet another one, two, or three hundred miles to the provincial capital, where, after wasting months, and spending all he had with him or could borrow in fees to lawyers and bribes to hangers-on of the courts, he, as likely as not, finally loses his case. Constituted as our civil courts are, the chances on each hearing do not preponderate largely in favour of real justice being done. What exactly the chances are of this happy event occurring three successive times in one case, I leave those, who make "the odds" their study, to calculate.

Winning or losing, he often returns utterly demoralised to his home; he has heard all the pleadings; quibbles and fictions on his side, quibbles and fictions on the other side; and he has listened to many other cases besides his own, and has been impressed with the fact that, on the whole, *dis*honesty is the best policy, and henceforth this conviction shapes his dealings with his banker and his neighbours. His banker on his part is in no way behind his debtor; indeed, having necessarily more to do with the courts, he earlier, as a rule, became a convert to the gospel of fraud; and the temptation to him was immense, for lands are saleable now, and the impossible rates of old bonds entered as a matter of form, when no one dreamt of repaying capital, are now enforcible, and the principal can be recovered too, and every landholder of every degree can be sold up out of house and home.

And perhaps our man is sold up, and the banker buys his land, and takes possession, and then—now and then the inherent love of his ancestral lands, his strongest passion, is too strong for the poor homeless wretch, and one evening in the dusk, when the unwary usurer, who has paid a visit to the village to see his new purchase, is wending his way homewards, there is a rush and the heavy thuds of a club, and the gallows ends the tragedy which our blundering philanthropy has so elaborately prepared.

And similarly, be it noticed, though it is a digression, that our laws and courts have set landlord against tenants, and converted too many of both classes into sad rogues. In the old days there was no talk of tenants-at-will, and tenants with occupancy rights, and so on. No doubt every landholder, where such really existed, *could* evict any tenant he chose, and if a man seduced his neighbour's wife (they were poor ignorant creatures), or otherwise insulted or offended the community, evicted he was, but custom barred, and far more effectively than any British law or court, any arbitrary exercise of this power, and the landlord who might any day have to defend his Penates against a Maratha inroad, an imperial functionary, or a band of dacoits, was obliged to keep good friends on the whole with the mass of his cultivators, on whose strong arms the safety of his property and the honour of his house might, at any moment, become dependent.

Both classes here, again, were bound together by ties of mutual obligation and inter-dependence, but we, with our ill-starred mania for exact systems of law, have dissolved the bonds, and have converted into antagonists the two great classes on whose harmonious co-operation not only their own welfare, but in many parts of the country the progress of our land revenue, so materially depends.

Let others write panegyrics on those who "first planted the seeds of a civilised system of jurisprudence in India": I, looking sadly now on the Upas tree that has crowned their labours, can only say:—

> Ille et nefasto te posuit die,
> Quicunque primum, et sacrilegâ manu,
> Produxit, arbos, in nepotum
> Perniciem, *opprobriumque pagi!*

No doubt it may startle some to propose that we should in these respects retrace our steps, and, eschewing the highly seasoned and artistic messes of civilisation, revert to the simple fruit and herbs of our unenlightened predecessors.

But the case stands thus:—The country is on the high road to bankruptcy: sudden and arbitrary reductions in all directions, not impossibly really wasting more money than they seem to save, will of course be resorted to, and a nominal equilibrium restored for a while.

No such measures, however, can restore the finances of a growing country to a healthy condition any more than cutting off strips from the ends of the legs to let in as gussets into the seat, is calculated to place the trousers of the growing boy in a permanently satisfactory condition.

He is bound to outgrow them, and the country is

bound to outgrow the existing revenue, snip and patch, botch and tinker as you will.

The only source from which you can derive that large increase of revenue which the empire must have hereafter if it is to continue to flourish, or even exist, is the land; and from the land this increase is not to be got so long as throughout wide provinces all classes of agriculturists are crippled by poverty and debt.

Some parts of the country are comparatively free from this blight. No measures that we decide to take need be universal in their application. In no two provinces, probably, would the remedy take precisely the same form, but broadly speaking, what is necessary wherever this disease has gained much ground, is to remove all cases connected with the money and grain transactions of agriculturists as such * from the cognisance of the regular courts, and secure the adjustment of all these by local tribunals.

Natives of known probity and fair intelligence (and in every province there are thousands of these, ignorant enough of law, but thoroughly able to settle fairly a money question between two other natives, when they have the real facts before them), such natives, we say, would be selected, many no doubt from our huge revenue establishments, and sent as judges, from village to village, to settle up, with the aid of the village elders, every case of debt of the

---

* Perhaps one in a thousand agriculturists is a trader as well as an agriculturist. With these and their trade transactions we need not concern ourselves.

kind referred to, in which any one of its inhabitants was concerned.

These judges would be fettered by no codes and no forms of procedure, and they would hear both parties' stories, *coram populo*, on the village platform of the debtor's own village. It is needless to tell any one who knows the country that while, when you get him into court, no witness seems to be *able* to tell the truth, on his own village platform, surrounded by his neighbours, no villager in personal questions like these seems able to tell an untruth. Everybody knows everybody else's affairs; let the speaker deviate perceptibly from the *facts*, and immediately out go tongues all round, and jeers and cries of "Wah," "Wah," remind him that he is *not* in court, and that that kind of thing will not go down at home.

The decisions thus passed would be final. Very likely some few of them would not be quite correct according to our ideas, but that signifies little; they would embody simple justice according to native ideas, and that is all we want; and even though a fraction did not do full justice according to even native ideas, we must accept some drawbacks in every arrangement, and, as every native says, better half justice at once than full justice after long delay and expensive litigation. Above all, even if in a few cases a partial failure of justice resulted, they would be absolutely insignificant in number as compared with those in which, under our present system, the failure is total.

Common sense would be the judge's sole guide. He would consider the merits of the case, the sum originally advanced, the payments made on account, the ordinary profits in regular (as opposed to speculative) trade in the neighbourhood, and either declare the debt discharged, or fix the amount still fairly due, and the interest, if any, thenceforth payable.

All this is in favour of the agriculturist; but, the decree given, the capitalist would no longer have to spend and spend, and petition and petition, to get it executed. The decree would be made over to the head revenue official* of the jurisdiction, whose duty it would be to see it realised, as an arrear of land revenue, as rapidly as was consistent with not ruining the debtor, without the money-lender taking any further trouble about the matter.

In some localities the state of the people is such that it would be desirable to set perhaps a hundred such judges to work for three months in a single district, assigning to each a circle of from ten to twenty villages according to population, and requiring the judges to adjust every such matter pending in each village, and voiding all claims not laid before them for adjustment. In other districts, again, one such judge for each pergunnah, tuppah, or other convenient local subdivision, or even one such for each tahsil or other local revenue circle would suffice, and it might not be necessary here to void claims not presented, but only to empower the judge to decide all cases brought before them by *either* party.

In many districts no immediate action seems called

---

* *Tahsildar* (Upper India); *Mooktearkar* (Sindh); *Mamlutdar* (Bombay), &c.

for, and most of those in which it is needed would be found to present minor peculiarities, requiring a corresponding adjustment of details. In some cases it would only be necessary to deal with the indebtedness of the landholders, in others only with that of the cultivators; while in some all classes of agriculturists need protection. All this would be for the decision of the local administrations in consultation with their revenue and agricultural officers; all that it is here pretended to give, is the cloth; if it is to wear well the coat must be carefully fitted in every instance.

The broad principles are, that whenever and wherever agricultural progress, on which the future welfare of the empire must, in a great measure, depend, is impeded or rendered impossible by the indebtedness of any or all classes of agriculturists, all questions connected with such indebtedness shall be removed from the cognisance of the civil courts, and their summary and final adjustment provided for by the instrumentality of respectable native judges versed in rural affairs, aided, but not governed, by the advice of the local elders in the village where the debtor resides; no fees of any kind to be paid; no stamps to be required; no pleaders or lawyers to be allowed to take any part in the transactions; decisions to be given effect to (equally without charge) by the revenue officials of the circle as speedily as is consistent with not ruining the debtor, and these officials to possess, in regard to amounts decreed, the same powers that they do in regard to arrears of land revenue. Adjustments once effected, arrangements to be made, either by the retention of a limited number of these rural judges or by other measures, to prevent a relapse.

It must be freely admitted that, under the proposed system, something like two-thirds of the existing total claims against agriculturists will probably be disallowed. In former days, when relations between money-lenders and agriculturists were less strained than they have now become in many places, the writer, taking advantage of his position and influence as district officer, has, as arbitrator, disposed, with the consent of both parties, of hundreds of such cases, precisely as he now proposes that the rural judges should be *empowered* to dispose of them.

Every case varies, and naturally some money-lenders are more honest, others more usurious; but it is believed that, taking a large series of such claims, it might be broadly asserted that, out of the sum total claimed, one-third was fairly due, one-third fairly enough put on to compensate for the uncertainties and intolerable delays and expenses (licit and illicit) of our courts, and that one-third was an inequitable charge due to exorbitant interest and compound interest.*

It would appear, therefore, that the proposed measure would be a great blow to the capitalist class, and that there might be danger, existing debts once cleared, of the money-lenders refusing to make new advances.

In the first place, once the people were fairly out of

---

* 24 to 30 per cent. are not at all unheard-of rates.

debt much fewer advances would be required, and the majority of these would not be to *save* ancestral holdings, but only to improve them; advances always more readily obtainable and at easier rates, because often made by classes of capitalists who will not deal with nearly ruined men.

In the second place, the native mofussil capital employed in usury is believed to be more than three-fold that employed in trade. By no possible means could the amount of the latter be more than doubled for many years, so that for a long time two-thirds at least of the capital now employed in money-lending in the mofussil *must* continue to be so employed.

In the third place, as a matter of fact (and this assertion is based on the repeated assertions of scores of village bankers in the Doab), many money-lenders would be perfectly content to have all their money out in agricultural advances at nine per cent. *if* they might make these at the village platform, before the rural judge, without going near any other court, without any bonds or stamps, and could then look for the recovery of any items not voluntarily repaid, to the revenue officers of the circle, and they would gladly let Government keep half per cent. of all it realised for them (and this would more than cover any expense incurred), and accept such slight losses as might prove inevitable.

It is necessary here to explain that losses, under such circumstances, would be rare in the extreme. Aside from the fatal lotteries of the civil courts, and dealt with in his own village, the Indian peasant is very honest, and he is still a great respecter of authority. Only death could prevent ninety-nine hundredths of our rural population paying a debt fairly incurred, on which a reasonable rate of interest was charged, and which they understood that the authorities required them to pay. And in the event of death, in nine cases out of ten, the heirs and representatives of the deceased who take up his land, would be quite as ready to take up the debt as if it were their own, and anyhow whoever took the land would have to take up the debt. In estates under the Court of Wards, not leased out but managed direct by revenue officials, large sums are often given out as advances, and again recovered to the uttermost fraction. Or when some loss is sustained by men dying, or others whose cattle have died, and whose crops have failed absconding,* this under good management is small.

Nor is it even *necessary*, though it is desirable, that there should be authority behind to sanction the debt. A gentleman, many years a planter in a district of which the writer had charge for a decade, remarked to him, speaking of cultivators :—

"Deal with them wisely and fairly, and there is no difficulty. I give out large advances every year. I have never had a suit in *any* court with any ryot, and

---

* As a rule it is *bad* management when men abscond. It is from fright they do so; they know they owe money; they find themselves, by some calamity, beggars; they do not know what the consequences may be, and they run away. Many a time, in wards' estates, have I sent some relative with a few rupees to re-assure and bring such men back, and many a time have I known others, who could not be traced, come back two, three, four, years later, with their whole debt, earned elsewhere, in their hands.

I have never lost any money worth speaking of. Misfortunes will happen, and you may have to wait and to do what sometimes looks like throwing good money after bad, but give them *time* and they will pay, if they feel you have always been on the square with them."

It may safely be asserted that it rests merely with us to redeem our people from the slavery of debt, and to ensure them a continuance of the enjoyment of the major portion of the capital hitherto available to them, and on *incomparably* easier and more satisfactory terms.

But it is conceivable that in some particular locality there might be a temporary *strike* of the money-lenders, and it is not only conceivable, but certain, that in some localities the Agricultural Department will find that the capital theretofore there available is wholly inadequate for the efficient working of the land.

So most certainly it is necessary to foresee the probability in *some* instances of Government having itself temporarily to undertake the duty of making advances.

Here it will perhaps be said that the system has already been tried and has failed. As a matter of fact, no real trial has ever been made, and it is, humanly speaking, certain that any properly made trial must succeed.

What has been done two or three times is this: Some district officer, already burthened with absolutely innumerable other duties, answerable to from twelve to twenty different superiors, each worrying his life out about his own section of the administration, has yet seen what was wanted and has asked permission to make advances. This has been accorded on a small scale, too small to pay its way, but still calculated to be of some use as an experiment. A beginning has been made, in one instance that I can recall in Oudh, on marvellously good lines, considering that the responsible officer had no time to give to the matter. Still his heart was in it, and at first something seemed to be coming of it. Long before any conclusion could be formed, the father of the scheme falls sick, or is promoted, or is transferred, and a new man comes who cares for none of these things; how many amongst us care to be bothered with other folks' trouble-giving children? Of course the scheme dies away.

Naturally I contemplate no such half-hearted peddling arrangements. The advances must be on a scale to pay for their administration, and the officer who makes them must have these and nothing else to attend to; it must be by these he makes or mars his reputation, stands or falls.

The agriculturist can well afford to pay nine per cent. for any money he wants. It is to him what money at three per cent would be to a farmer at home.

With no courts, no stamps, no bonds, nine per cent. will, if work is done on a considerable scale, pay all expenses of management, all *losses*, and return at least a clear six per cent.

It is not even possible that Government should have to undertake this business generally; it will only be in some special localities that its intervention will be needed. Nor is it contemplated that it should anywhere *permanently* carry it on; there are political objections to an alien Government becoming the universal creditor. Men are but men, and when the debt grew burthensome and hard to be repaid, there might be a tendency to seize the sponge of rebellion and wipe out the foreign creditor. And, indeed, even from the first it is probable that much of the capital required for these rural banks could be obtained locally from natives on a guarantee of six per cent., the money only to be called for as required, and to be repayable at any time. Great native bankers even have repeatedly assured the writer, that when money was perfectly safe, and there was no chance of courts or other trouble, they were well satisfied to have a portion of their money out at six per cent. And by a little tact in dealing with the subscribers, utilising their local knowledge, giving them a sort of voice in the management of affairs, and so paving the way for it, there is no doubt that after a time Government would be able to drop out of these rural banks, leaving them in the hands of partners or associations, and retaining no responsibility except for keeping up the rural judges, before whom the advances would be made, and who would settle disputes about them, (and once the system was in force there would be few of these,) and for giving effect, as above described, to the judge's decisions.

But we must not pursue further this inexhaustible subject; suffice it if we have conveyed some idea of the more prominent features of this great obstacle to agricultural reform, and have afforded some indication of the direction in which remedies may be sought.

There is another large, and in Upper India very pressing, question which *must* have the early attention of the Agricultural Department. We have already described the progress and explained the inevitable future results of that insidious saline efflorescence known locally as "*reh.*" No one can doubt that one of two measures is essential—either give up all hopes of making canals pay, and only allow irrigation, in localities where the soil is favourable to the formation of this pest, once or twice in every ten or eleven years, in other words, in seasons of severe drought, or lower the level of your head of water, reduce your subsoil water level, allow only irrigation by lift and none by flow, and have recourse to subsoil drainage.

So little is generally understood of the natural properties of soils that here in India, at any rate, two strong objections are often raised to subsoil drainage:—

1*st.*—That the soils are poor enough and light enough as they are, and that to encourage the water to run through them as a sieve, would in two or three years ensure all "the goodness" being washed out of them.

2*nd.*—That where "*reh*" is concerned, all subsoil drainage could do would be to draw into the soil what is now on the surface, and make matters worse.

The answer, as all agriculturists know, is complete. Without trenching on debateable ground, and avoiding the details of this very difficult question, it may be stated that, so far from water passing through the soil being able to wash out of it "the goodness," the soil exercises the most powerful attraction over the food constituents of plants, and not only retains those existing in it but seizes these out of solutions passing through it. Thus phosphoric acid, potash, ammonia, and (except in soils very poor in lime) silicic acid, the most important of the food elements, obtained from the soil, cannot normally be washed out of it by any amount of subsoil drainage; on the contrary, the soil acts like a filter to arrest these and decomposes solutions containing these which pass through it in order to retain them.

Of course there are limitations, most prominent amongst which is the fact that for each soil there seems to be a point of saturation, if we may use the word, of each food constituent; up to that point the soil seizes all it can get of that element; beyond that point it allows it to pass away in solution. Nothing is more greedily seized by most soils than potash, but you may get bog-earths that allow potash solutions to pass through them untouched.

Of course, you may raise the point of saturation for any element by adding more of some other element, but this is in effect changing the soil. For *each* soil the point of saturation for each food constituent is liable to vary.

Other minerals, not useful to plant-life, pass freely in solution through the soil, and food constituents even, when by the chemistry of the soil they have assumed forms useless as the food of plants, or forms of which there is already a full supply, pass away.

So while by subsoil drainage our soils will lose* no appreciable percentage of plant food not already stored therein up to their maximum retention capacity, all the excess salts now lying thick on the surface will be redissolved, carried down through the soil, so far as needed, decomposed therein, all useful portions retained which are necessary to make up the full capital stock that the particular soil can hold, and the excess together with useless or injurious matter passed away with the drainage water.

Varying as does the composition of this always complex saline efflorescence, in different localities† very different additions to the soil, organic or mineral, may be necessary to enable it to seize the maximum share of the utilisable portions of the "*reh*" when by subsoil drainage it is filtered downwards.

All these are details which must be worked out by experiment on scientific principles; the broad truth remains that save under, for India, exceptional circumstances, the only practicable mode of purifying land now sterilised by this "*reh*," or protecting land in course of being so sterilised, is by passing the excess of saline matters away by subsoil drainage.

It is needless to add that, independent of this special evil, subsoil drainage, and the deep working and oxidization of the soil that it involves, by multiplying

---

* In solution, of course, is meant; *mechanically*, anything may, by bad arrangements, be *swept* away.

† Lime, soda, potassium, magnesia, as carbonates, chloride, sulphates, nitrites, and nitrates, all occur, but the soda salts are usually the chief constituents, and the nitrites and nitrates are scarce.

many fold the area of storage of moisture and food constituents available to the crops, must in the case of many* soils exercise a most powerful influence in controlling the ravages of drought.

The great difficulty with us, where subsoil drainage is most required, is to obtain a suitable outfall, but this again, like so many of the points touched on in the foregoing remarks, is just one of those questions that we require an Agricultural Department to thresh out thoroughly.

Innumerable other minor matters naturally suggest themselves as falling within the scope of the Agricultural Department.

One not unimportant point is economy in seed grain. It is astonishing what an enormous amount of grain is wasted in most parts of the country in over-seeding, the result being a poorer and lighter crop than if one-third of the quantity had been used as seed. It ought not to be difficult to bring this gradually home to the minds of the masses.

The unquestionable improvement in the size, strength, and condition of the major portion of the cattle when relieved of the cruel yearly fast which now so certainly dwarfs the young, and injures permanently the stamina of the adults, has been already

---

* In the preceding remarks I have endeavoured to avoid putting forward partial as absolute truths. Yet I feel that even now there is scarcely a sentence that does not require further limitations and qualifications to make it *accurate;* but how is it possible to convey in a couple of pages *truly* accurate ideas on such subjects? A general, if rather hazy, bird's-eye view, neglecting all but the most prominent features, is all that can be hoped for.

alluded to. Few realise how great this *improvement* would be; the writer has out of pure pity taken almost moribund calves out of skeleton herds, to turn them out, three or four years later, double the weight and almost half as big again as any adult in the herd from which they sprung. Ensure the existing herds sufficient food all the year round for a dozen years, and the whole aspect of our cattle will have changed. But it is not therefore contended that much besides this may not be done to improve the breed in many places by an infusion of a superior strain. On the contrary, there is no question that this will have to be done. There are whole provinces in which the climate is less favourable to cattle than that of others, and where the constant infusion of new blood will be necessary to maintain a fine breed. There are limited tracts again where the cattle are perhaps, for the purposes for which we require them, second to none in the world, and clearly the diffusion of these fine strains will become a necessity later. And perhaps the Agricultural Department may improve on these even by judicious crossing,

It must here, however, be noticed, for the mistake is often made, that the last cross we require is with prize English cattle. At home they have for generations bred for meat and milk. We want to breed for work.

If existing domestic breeds do not suffice (and they are very numerous and some of them very fine), then further efforts should be made to obtain crosses from the magnificent indigenous wild stocks (the Gaur and the Mithun, *Bos gaurus* and *Bos frontalis*), grand beasts that stand seventeen hands high, whose rush is like that of a broad-gauge express, and who yet scamper over rocks and ravines almost like goats.

Greater cleanliness in harvesting, and greater care in separating grains* and seeds intended for or likely to reach foreign markets, would probably do much to improve the demand for our agricultural products, and doubtless some endeavours will be made by the Agricultural Department to impress this on the people, both by precept and by example at their own farms, but this is typical of a whole class of reforms, on which it is needless to touch, as they must mainly be brought about by private enterprise and by the pressure of purchasers. Could we only secure a fairly steady and moderately large export trade in wheat and barley, for instance, there is no doubt that in a very few years the better prices given by the purchasing agents of exporting firms would effect a complete change in the existing slovenly practices, but unfortunately it would seem that, at any rate until the more easily accessible virgin lands of Western America are more or less exhausted (and they do appear to be exhausting these in a wickedly wasteful manner), it will only be under favour of bad seasons elsewhere, or of wars interfering with the natural course of trade, that our wheat is likely to find a wide European market.†

---

* It is not merely that grains of two species should not be muddled up together as now, but that the different qualities of each grain, *e.g.* red and white, soft and hard wheat, and the like, should be kept distinct.

† It has, however, been asserted that a great deal of this wheat has been put into the European market below its cost

Again, as typical of another class of duties which the Department would undertake, but of which little need here be said (so obviously do they fall within its province) may be instanced, the improvement of staples, both by disseminating the better existing indigenous varieties in tracts where now only inferior ones are cultivated, and by further improving the best existing sorts by selection* and careful cultivation.

But among the secondary objects of the Department, not perhaps so obvious, may certainly be mentioned the improvement of agricultural implements and mechanical appliances. The magnificent mechanical developments of European scientific agriculture are, and will for many generations probably remain, utterly unsuited to Indian requirements. On the other hand, the indigenous appliances that here do duty for these, are of the crudest and most inefficient character. Improvements in these are urgently called for, but they have yet to be created, and this not by the bodily importation of the results achieved by

---

price, having been carried in America at nominal rates in consequence of certain railway combinations. In the absence of particulars, it is impossible to say whether this can appreciably affect our future trade.

* The word "selection" is here used in its widest sense, and is not intended only to signify the picking out for seed purposes the biggest grains out of the finest ears and the like. It is meant to include the careful study of varieties, with reference to local conditions, and the further development of peculiarities which in any locality tend to diminish the chance of the failure of the crop or increase its probable yield. Take, for instance, the Long-husked Giant Millet (or *Choncha Jowar*), which is even now almost proof against the attacks of crows, mainas, and the like, and which a very slight further development of its peculiarity would render absolute proof against all birds but parroquets.

science in Europe, but by the application of the principles on which those results are based to the widely different conditions and requirements of this country. Of these, the people who pester Government to purchase grand combined steam ploughing, reaping and threshing machines for the ryots here, seem to have about as accurate a conception as a certain Maharajah, who was with difficulty dissuaded from sending home an elephant to an old pensioner at Bayswater (who complained of being no longer able to get about on foot and being too poor to keep a conveyance), had of those of our London suburbs.

Perhaps next to ploughs, in regard to which Mr. Buck has already done something (and if we had half a dozen provincial Directors, each aided by proper mechanical engineers, and each improving on the improvements of his neighbours, we should soon get the very thing wanted), next we say to ploughs, no mechanical appliances will more emphatically demand the study of the Department than those for raising water by wind-power. Assuming, as we may, that as the Agricultural Department obtains a real hold upon the country, high-level canals rendering subsoil drainage impossible, and involving the gradual sterilisation of the soil, wherever this is at all appreciably impregnated with saline substances, will become things of the past, and assuming, too, that irrigation on a rational system will be largely developed, the importance of cheap and efficient contrivances for raising water becomes obvious.

And for cheapness, in a country like India where, over whole provinces, winds blow with almost the regularity of clockwork, probably no motive power could compare with that of wind.

At present a gigantic wind-power (second only to the equally unutilised sun-ray power) is running to waste, utterly uncared for over the whole empire, and any successful application of this to the purposes of irrigation would inaugurate a new era in the history of Indian Agriculture.

But it never was intended in this paper to enter into details like these, or to attempt even in the most preliminary fashion an exhaustive sketch of the work which lies before a real working Department of Agriculture in India. On the contrary, although we may even now form certain general conceptions of some of the problems awaiting its investigations, it will not be until years after its establishment that the Department itself will be in a position to set out the majority of these problems with that precision and fulness which is essential to any scientific method of solution.

After all, despite the attempts that have been made in this paper to give a somewhat more definite, and to the ordinary mind, more satisfactory reply, the best answer to the question—"For what do we need an Agricultural Department in India?"—must still remain,—firstly, to ascertain *precisely* what reforms are essential in our existing agriculture, as practised in various parts of the empire; secondly, to work out systematically the best methods of carrying through these reforms.

APPENDIX.

Note A.

(*Extract from an unpublished Memoir on the Agriculture of the Duáb, written in* 1859–60.)

SEASONS.

Our European calendar year, which is based on the true tropical year, or the interval between two successive arrivals of the sun at the vernal equinox, provides for the return of the seasons on which depend all agricultural operations on the same dates, year after year.

Not so the native calendar, which is alone in general use amongst our up-country agriculturists. They have, it is true, a *Sourburkh* or solar year of 365 days, and *Sourmas* or solar months; but these, though referred to by the Pundits in calculating horoscopes, and fixing auspicious days and seasons for marriages and the like, are dead letters to the rural population, who universally, in every-day practice, deal only with a lunar year of 12* months, consisting of between 354 and 355 days. This year being more than ten days shorter than the tropical year, a thirteenth month, known as *Lond* or *Adhikmas*, has to be intercalated every 32 or 33 months, and a variety of other corrections (which I once knew, but have

* These 12 lunar months, of about 29 days and 12¾ hours, which reckon from new moon to new moon, *i.e.* from the moon leaving its conjunction with the sun to its return to conjunction, must not be confounded with the periods (of about 27 days 7¾ hours) at the end of which the moon returns to a position *amongst the stars* nearly coincident with that it held at the commencement of such period.

now forgotten) have to be applied; the result of which is, that the seasons do not recur year after year on the same dates, or even in the same months.

The consequence of this non-conformity is that, as a rule, agricultural operations are, so far as any calendar goes, chiefly governed by what our villagers call *nakhats*, and the Pundits *nichattr*; properly speaking, I believe, *nakshattra*. These *nakhats* are nothing but subdivisions of the Zodiac, of which there are 27 in all, or 2¼ in each "*burj*" or sign, and their names are given to the periods during which the sun's apparent path lies within them. Of course by the slow effects of precession and nutation, the seasons in which these *nakhats* fall *very slowly* change, but practically they are sufficiently immutable for every-day life, and cultivators commonly enquire about them from the Pundits, regulate their sowings not a little by them, and have the firmest belief in certain traditional prognostications, favourable and unfavourable, to their crops, dependent on what happens during their course.

With the 15 *nakhats* that lie between about the 27th November and 23rd May we need not concern ourselves, as one hears comparatively little of the good or evil influence of these; but the 12 *nakhats* which begin about the 23rd May play an important part, according to our agriculturists, in all their operations, and must be separately noticed.

1. Rohinee.—From about* the 23rd May to the 5th June. In this period, say the people, the rains should commence, and this is the time to sow maize, *oorud* (*Phaseolus Roxburghii*)—*murrooa* (*Eleusine coracana*). The native couplet runs—

> "Rohinee mirgsir boö mukkha
> Oordh, Murrooa, deo na taka":

"Sow maize and māsh (or oorud) and millets in Rohinee or Mirgsir, but, pay no rent."

2. Mirgsir.—From about the 6th to the 19th June. In this period also the crops above mentioned are sown, but if much rain falls during it, neither *jowar* (*Sorghum vulgare*) nor cotton must be sown, otherwise, when they come to flower, insects will surely attack them; the only consolation being that if it rains well in *Ootra nakhat* (*vide infra*) the insects will disappear. *Panicum milliaceum*, though generally a hot-weather crop with us, is said

* Owing to differences in the calendars, the *nakhats* do not always begin on *exactly* the same European dates, sometimes *Rohinee*, for instance, begins on the 22nd May.

to succeed specially well if sown at this time. I have never seen it grown at this season, but the proverb runs:—

> " Mirgsir men boö chena,
> Zemindar ko kuch mut dena" :

" Sow chena* in Mirgsir, give nothing to the zemindar."

3. Adra.—From about 20th June to the 4th July. This is the great sowing season, and if only sufficient rain falls at this time, the majority of the autumnal crops are got in. For *til* (*Sesamum orientale*), *jowar* (*Sorghum vulgare*), *urhur* (*Cajanus indicus*), *moth* (*Phaseolus mungo*), *moong* (*P. mungo*), cotton, *Rousa* or *Lobeea* (*Dolichos sinensis*), *kulthi* or *koortee* or *bhutwas* (*D. uniflorus*), *oorud* or *mash* (*P. Roxburghii*), *suman* (*Panicum miliare*), *kuknee* (*P. italicum*), and some others of the lesser millets, this is *the* time *par excellence*, but *bajera* (*Penicillaria spicata*) is said not to succeed if sown in this *nakhat*. If there is no rain at this time, the yield, both of cotton and *jowar*, is seriously endangered.

4. Poonbursoo.—From about the 5th to the 17th July. This and the next following *nakhat* are the favourite sowing times for rice; the legend runs:—

> " Pookh, Poonbursoo bowe dhan
> Aslaikha ko do din parmán" :

" Poonbursoo, Pookh, and two days of Aslaikha are best for sowing rice." *Bajera* is also sown to some extent during this period.

5. Pookh.—From about the 18th July to the 1st August. This is the best time for sowing *bajera*, and rice that could not be got in in Poonbursoo is sown now.

> " Boö bajera aye Pookh,
> Phir man mate bhogo sookh."

In other words, if you want things to go happily sow your bajera when *Pookh* appears.

6. Aslaikha.—From about the 2nd to the 15th August. *Kodon* (*Paspalum scrobiculatum*) is generally sown at this time. Heavy rain during this period is considered very injurious, and clear weather during its continuance is greatly preferred. If it does rain, the cultivators never allow the water to lie in the fields (except perhaps in those of rice and sugar-cane), but drain it off or bale it out most perseveringly. You may sometimes see every man, woman, and child in a village hard at work at this. If the

---

* This is the common native name for *P. miliaceum*, and is of course quite different from *chunna*, which is the ordinary gram.

water be allowed to lie, the crops turn yellow, and even if they do not rot, yield a much smaller harvest.

7. MUGHA.—From about the 16th to the 29th August. This is considered the most critical time of the year, and good rains are devoutly prayed for. The people say:—

"Mugha ke burse,
Mata ke purse":

"The rains of Mugha are like mother's milk."

Not only does the *kharif* or autumn crop greatly depend on good rains at this time, but many of the *rabi* or spring staples, and most especially gram, are thought to be materially influenced for the better by really good heavy rain. At this time good rains in this *nakhat* make up for most previous shortcomings; as the people say "Chhoot khet ootur jata hai," "The failings of the fields disappear." The only exceptions are, *til* (*Sesamum orientale*) and other oil seeds; in their case it is asserted that if it rains without stopping during the first five days of Mugha, insects are sure later to attack the plants. The water of this *nakhat*, unlike that of the preceding one, is commonly allowed to lie in the fields, and is said to be specially beneficial to many of the millets and pulses. On the whole this is the period on which, according to the cultivators, most depends:—

"Jo kahin Mugha burse jul,
Sub najon men honge phul":

"If only Mugha gives us rain,
Every field will teem with grain."

8. POORBA.—From about the 30th August to the 11th September. Rain at this time is considered injurious; if the weather is clear, blight and insects rarely do much harm, but if there is much rain, they make sad havoc of the crops:—

"Jo kahin Poorba pani dewen,
Jinson sub ko keera khawen":

"Whenever Poorba brings us rain,
In every crop, worms mar the grain."

9. OOTTRA.—From about the 12th to the 25th September. Rain during this period is most desirable; the crops make great progress, and where insects have attacked the plants, they disappear. The legend goes that if there is good rain at this time, the harvest will be so plentiful that even the dogs will be too satiated with grain to eat it.

"Jub bursenga Oottra
Naj na khawen kootra":

10. HUST.—From about the 26th September to the 8th October. If there has been no rain in the previous period, it is anxiously looked for now, and under any circumstances, though rain at this time may injure some of the *kharif* crops, it will be most beneficial for the *rabi.*

11. CHITTRA.—From about the 9th to the 22nd October. If the two previous *nakhats* have passed without rain, and there is much rain in this one, the *kharif* is reckoned as lost, and apprehensions of scarcity, if not famine, become serious. Although thus injurious to the *kharif*, it promises well for all the *rabi* crops, except barley (which it is said to injure), and this, I think, is the purport of the traditional couplet:—

> "Oottra, ootur de gaeen, Hust gae mookh more,
> Jae jo kuheeo Chittra se, gae sumae lao buhore":

"Oottra's come and gone again. Hust has passed with face averted. Go, prithee, and bid Chittra bring a missing harvest back again."

12. SWANT.—From about the 23rd October to the 4th November. Rain at this period is most injurious to the majority of the autumn crops. Cotton it almost ruins if heavy; indeed the legend says:—

> "Jo bursen Poonurbus Swant,
> Chule na churka, buji na tant":

"If both Poonurbus rain and Swant, spindles and looms alike stand still."

Jowar loses its flavour, and the grain turns a reddish brown. *Bajera* yields but little, and that little very often so indurated as to be nearly useless. As for the "musemah," as the pulses (*oordh, moong, moth, rousa*) are collectively called, insects attack and more or less seriously injure them.

My own personal experience does not lead me to place *implicit* confidence in these standing prognostications (of which, by the way, I have only noted a few of the most important), but they are so generally believed in by our cultivators that it was impossible to overlook them in even the briefest sketch of the existing state of agriculture, and they may possibly embody more or less substantially correct generalisations from the experience of bygone ages. I have given only the existing popular versions, but the Prakrit originals are known to some Pundits.

All these prognostications refer, as will have been seen, to that agriculturally pre-eminently important portion of the year lying between the beginning of June and the end of October, which includes the periodical* rains; and, indeed, it is only natural that in a country like the plains of the Duáb the cultivator's chief source of anxiety should be the rains; for though the extension of canals is slightly changing the position of affairs, a bad rainy season still means a bad harvest, high prices, and scarcity; and a good one, plenty and comparative comfort to all classes.

It is hardly necessary to say that, with so much at stake, an ignorant and superstitious people have recourse to a variety of ceremonies, both to ensure success to their cultivation and to ascertain, beforehand, their prospects. The taking of omens (*shegoon*) is universally practised, the full moon of *Asarh* (generally in June) being one of the great days for this. The methods adopted are very various, but the most popular are those based on the direction of the wind at the time of the full moon of Asarh, *Pun purchutea* as it is termed. The cultivators assemble in some open plain, collect a little finely-powdered earth, and throw it up in the air. If the dust drifts northwards, the omen is bad, and insufficient rains are expected; if southwards, westwards or eastwards, it is favourable. Sometimes, instead of earth, raw cotton is loosely twisted into a thread and tied to the end of a bamboo (this is called *Dhujabundee*), and the direction of the wind ascertained from this. In all cases, a south, south-east, or south-west wind at this time is considered to indicate bad rains and a poor harvest. This is only one class of omen. All kinds of absurd practices are in vogue; for instance, at this same full moon, a few ounces of grain are carefully weighed, and are placed in little earthen saucers, in some open and elevated place well away from the village. Next morning the grain (if any remains, *my* experience being that it is generally eaten during the night) is carefully weighed; if it has gained weight the cultivator is sanguine of a good harvest; if it has lost, then he looks for a poor crop; if it has disappeared altogether, *then* the harvest will be as God wills.

Ridiculous as these superstitions must seem, they deserve notice, because cultivators are often governed in their choice of crops for the coming season by the result of these omens, and because it is impossible to introduce any improved system of agriculture without realising the extent to which the present practice of the art is governed by superstition.

---

* The periodical rains of the rainy season, which occur between Asarh and Kwar, say from June to October, are called "Chomas," while the cold-weather showers, which ought to occur about Christmas, are known as the "Mahawut."

Note B.

Some matters Agricultural and Horticultural in which the Department of Agriculture has been able to assist.

One step towards the development of agricultural and industrial enterprise in India certainly consists in the collection and dissemination of useful information. There has always been a good deal of information on record on matters connected with this important subject, but scattered and hidden in public offices and elsewhere, undigested, fragmentary, incomplete, and vague. One of the first objects of the Department was to gather up all this information, collect fresh facts by special enquiry, co-ordinate the whole, bring the facts down to the latest date, and publish them in a handy and useful way for general information. Amongst the papers published in accordance with this plan are the following:—

1. An account of silk.
2. A report on tobacco.
3. A note on lac.
4. A note on vanilla.
5. A note on flax.
6. A note on the *Eucalyptus globulus*, or blue gum of Australia.
7. A note on the various other species of *Eucalyptus* adapted to cultivation in India.
8. A note on *Ceratonia siliqua*, the carob tree.
9. A note on *Calophyllum inophyllum*, an oil-producing tree.
10. A note on *Malachra capitata*, an excellent fibre, quite neglected as yet.
11. A note on the *Arachis hypogœa* (the ground nut).
12. A note on *Sorghum saccharatum*, a valuable fodder.
13. A note on Cardamom cultivation.
14. A manual of Cinchona cultivation in India.

Others are still under preparation in the Department:

15. On dyes and tans.
16. On fibres, with special reference to paper-making.
17. On Carolina rice.
18. On wheat.
19. On Manilla hemp.

Some of the Local Governments have followed the example thus set, and under their instructions reports on jute, tea, tobacco, and cotton have been compiled by local officers. In the N.-W. P. especially the local Department of Agriculture and Commerce has issued notes on economic minerals, gums and resins, and dyestuffs, and a Dictionary of Agriculture is under preparation. In Madras a text-book of Agriculture has been compiled by Mr. Robertson, but in these two provinces alone has the example and encouragement given by the Department for the compilation of agricultural text-books been of any practical use.

Actual experiments have been undertaken in the cultivation of most of the articles on which papers have been published, and in many cases the results have been very successful. In tobacco, for instance, but little more remains to be done by the Government, an energetic European firm having undertaken the cultivation and manufacture of it on good principles in farms made over to the firm for the purpose (they were old stud farms) on very favourable terms by the Government.

In silk, experiments with tasar have been a complete success, and there is undoubtedly a splendid future for the trade in this article, little known or appreciated, out of India, until this Department moved in the matter.

Experiments in the propagation of lac have been quite successful, but a fall in prices in the foreign markets renders the further prosecution of this business for the present unnecessary.

The cultivation of vanilla, so profitable in Mexico and Réunion, a trial of which in India was strongly urged by this Department, was a success in one province, at any rate, until the occurrence of a drought which desolated it. This article offers peculiar advantages to those who would wish to derive profit from an ornamental plant occupying little space, and which may be grown in the garden adjoining the house.

The carob tree, though long previously introduced, has also, by the instrumentality of this Department, been largely propagated, and this useful fodder tree and resource for human beings in seasons of drought (as in Cyprus) may now, like the Australian gums, be considered naturalised in India.

The ground nut is extensively imported into France from the west coast of Africa, and this article, which is well known in India, though not regularly exported, may become an important trade, if properly worked. So far as exhortations and the supply of information goes, this Department has done its best to stimulate the cultivation of this valuable product.

Sorgho has done remarkably well. Its very heavy yield makes it a most valuable crop for cattle food. Year after year this Department has imported and distributed the seed, has directed and encouraged the experimental culture of the plant, and has collected from the growers, and compiled and published records of the results.

Cinchona is now completely established in India, and the alkaloid prepared from the bark is largely used in the hospitals and in private practice.

The introduction of the cinchona was due to others, but to the persistent efforts of this Department is mainly due the fact, that we have now an excellent and efficient febrifuge, little, if at all, inferior to the sulphate of quinine, which can be, and is, sold retail in every bazar at R. 1 (or say 1*s.* 9*d.*) the ounce.

The results of numerous experiments made with Carolina rice, another staple of which this Department has, year after year, imported and widely distributed, large quantities of the best seed, are still indecisive, but the trials are being continued. This rice is far superior to the finest rice now grown in India, and is worth, in the London market, double the price of the best Bengal rice.

Many of these experiments were tried in the so-called model and experimental farms established under instructions from, or by the advice and with the encouragement of, the Department. Of these farms, there were eight last year, viz. at Allahabad, Cawnpore, Nagpore, in Khandesh, in Sind, at Bangalore, in Madras, and in Burma. There were also two old stud farms which were made over on favourable terms to a European firm for the cultivation and manufacture of tobacco on an improved system. One of these was at Ghazipore, and another at Poosah.

No doubt several of these farms were so managed as to exhibit rather what to avoid, than what to imitate, but located in bad sites, and managed by people who had no real knowledge of farming, all the Department could do was to get such little good out of them as it could, and try and keep things a little straight by means of remarks, criticisms, and suggestions on the reports periodically received.

The necessity for a proper system for the management of such farms, and the need for the creation of agricultural schools, working in connection with them has been, time after time, emphatically pointed out to the local Governments in letters and resolutions, and close attention to the subject has been earnestly commended to them. Without the co-operation of the local Governments no sort of progress could be made as matters stood, seeing that, under the scheme of provincial finance, the whole cost of farms and agricultural schools has to be borne by provincial revenues.

In these farms experiments have been tried with new crops as well as crops known in the country, under different conditions and in different soils, the results being carefully recorded, and trials have been made of improved implements of every kind, ploughs, pumps, hoes, &c. Of course the principle to observe is that the lighter, simpler, and cheaper such implements are, the greater is the chance of their adoption by native agriculturists, and this the Department has ever sought to impress on all concerned.

Of experiments conducted under orders from the Department,

or with its concurrence and encouragement, the following may be noticed:—

Trials have been made to establish the relative cost of growing wheat and oats, with reference to communications from the Military Department, suggesting the extended cultivation of oats for the feed of troop horses. It is believed that oats cost as much to grow as wheat, and that the crop is not nearly as remunerative, and the trials were intended to verify these points.

Trials have been made in the North-Western Provinces and the Punjab with a description of rice much grown in Sikkim, which requires no irrigation. Such rice would be very useful in many localities.

The value of poudrette, as a manure, has been made the subject of innumerable and most careful experiments. Other manures have also been tried from time to time, but it is unnecessary to refer to them, seeing that for a considerable time to come the principal manures within the reach of the agricultural population of India will be farm-yard manure, crushed bones, and poudrette, and against the use of the latter there are caste prejudices still to be overcome.

At one time a blight threatened the utter destruction of the opium crop of Behar. Appearing season after season over a constantly increasing area, grave apprehensions were entertained as to the prospects of the important revenue depending on this crop. A minute and searching scientific investigation into the blight was undertaken under the advice of this Department by a very competent observer, Mr. John Scott, of the Calcutta Botanic Gardens, and this investigation, carried on over a period of some five years, has resulted in proving that the "blight" is due to a vicious system of cultivation. The seed is never changed or selected, the soil has been exhausted, and the plants have degenerated and die from disease induced by exhaustion. The vices of the system of opium cultivation are, in fact, the vices which affect Indian agriculture generally.

In Port Blair, also under the advice, and in most cases at the instance, of this Department, experiments have been made with Sea-island cotton, tobacco, vanilla, coffee, and Manilla hemp, in every case with more or less success, although the existing condition of the settlement prevents the success being followed up on a large scale.

Experiments were tried with the sunflower, which is largely cultivated as an oil-producer in Russia, and which was reported (erroneously) to possess a malaria-destroying capacity; but, after a year or so of comparative failure, it was concluded that it was more to the purpose to increase and stimulate the production and improve the quality of articles already well known in the country than to grow crops of which the ultimate commercial success was doubtful. Amongst such articles may be instanced the ground nut (*Arachis hypogæa*), already referred to, and careful enquiries having been made, a paper has been circulated recommending it to the attention of cultivators and merchants.

Malachra capitata is another indigenous article in which experiments have been made expressly at the instance of the Department. This fibre has been pronounced to be equal to jute, and growing as it does without particular care and capable of cultivation at less cost than jute, it is a fibre which will probably prove of great economic importance to Bombay.

The improvement of the indigenous paper manufacture, and the provision of cheap fibres suitable for paper-making, has engaged much attention in this Department. A treatise on the subject has been for some years in course of preparation, and would long since have been published but for the necessity of awaiting the results of the experiments now being carried out in Bengal, Burmah, &c. in regard to bamboos, at Mr. Routledge's instance, and on a variety of coarse reeds and grasses.

Other fibres, too, have engaged attention, such as the Agave, the wild plantain fibre of the Andamans, and the *Musa textilis*, producing what is known as Manilla hemp. But chief of all the fibres of India, the best fibre in the world in fact, is the rheea or ramie. This Department has, since 1871, perseveringly tried to obtain a machine adapted for the separation of the fibre from the bark, the existing manual process making the fibre too expensive for ordinary use. A reward of 50,000 rupees was offered for such a machine or process, and the best machine produced having been found, though meritorious in some respects, not adapted for ordinary use, the offer of a reward was renewed, further competition invited, and a public trial is to be held in September, at which it seems probable that the question at issue will be solved.

Besides sorgho, successful trials have been made of another valuable forage plant (*Reana luxurians*), which may be said to be now completely naturalised. The solid-stemmed comfrey, another capital cattle food introduced by this Department, seems to be doing admirably in the Himalayas at elevations of from 3,000 to 7,000 feet.

Great attention has been given to the cultivation of ipecacuanha (another invaluable specific for one of the most fatal of tropical diseases), the introduction of which into India this Department was the first to take vigorously in hand.

Tobacco, to which allusion has already been made, has been carefully tried in many places, and good exotic seed repeatedly imported from Havana, Manilla, and the United States, and widely distributed. Arrangements have also been made for a regular series of analyses of Indian tobacco by the Government Quinologist at Calcutta.

Cochineal was imported from Teneriffe, and tried at Bangalore, but failed, apparently in consequence of defects in the local management.

The experiments made in silk of the mulberry worm, as well as the tasar worm, are full of promise, and, as regards the latter, the only question now really remaining to be solved is whether cocoons can be procured in quantity sufficient to meet the demand within the limit of price which European reelers can afford to give.

The cultivation of cotton on the Egyptian system, and that of Liberian coffee, have both been tried with success.

Endeavours have been made, but as yet without success, to obtain efficient rice-hulling machines, which would be very useful in some parts of the country.

On the other hand, the attempts which have repeatedly been made to foist elaborate agricultural machinery on the people have been systematically discouraged. In a poor country like India, where the rate of wage is extremely low and the holdings much sub-divided, the labour-saving machinery, which is invaluable in England and the United States, would be utterly useless.

A system, not originating, however, with this Department, has been cordially supported and sanctioned as an experiment under which, in certain districts, the State will construct wells for agriculturists, the cost being repaid to the State by instalments.

Similarly, though not sanguine of success, this Department has supported sheep-breeding in Burma, experimental farms having been started at Thyet Myo and Rangoon, aided by a grant from imperial revenues of 6,000 rupees for five years. Cattle have also been bred on Diamond Island and Table Island. Cattle-breeding in Mysore and horse-breeding in the Punjab have been encouraged, and in Oudh, as also in Burma, a qualified veterinary surgeon was deputed for some time to train native salutris (veterinary practitioners) to treat cattle properly when attacked by disease. The experiment, considering the minute scale on which it was tried, has been very fairly successful.

The appointment of a Cattle Plague Commission to investigate and report upon the subject of cattle disease in India elicited a voluminous report from the Commission. The establishment of a Veterinary College, which project arose out of the proceedings of the Commission, was frustrated, as stated in another part of this paper, and there was no practical outcome of the work of the Commission, except a handy manual of the more deadly forms of cattle disease, of which this Department directed the preparation; a most useful work, which was widely distributed, and translations of which, into the vernaculars of the country, were circulated extensively amongst the agricultural community.

This manual describes the more deadly forms of plague so plainly and clearly that any man may recognise the form of disease from which his unhealthy stock is suffering; it also prescribes the treatment to be applied for cure as well as the measures necessary to prevent infection and to keep cattle in health.

In arboriculture the introduction or extended propagation of the following trees, some of which have been already noticed, has been effected or stimulated, in every case (except that of cork-oak, which is as yet doubtful) with more or less complete success: Mahogany, baobab, caoutchouc-yielding trees and plants, carob, *Eucalyptus globulus* and other Australian gums, prosopis of kinds, Spanish chestnut, cork-oak, algarroba, and the Arabian date palm.

In many of these cases the initiative came from elsewhere, but in every case this Department assisted and promoted every reasonable proposal so far as was possible without any machinery of its own, and with the very limited means at its disposal.

London: Printed by W. H. Allen & Co., 13 Waterloo Place.